COPENHAGEN

FROM ABOVE

Forlaget Globe

COPENHAGEN

FROM ABOVE

Photos: Henrik Schurmann

Text: Claus Hagen Petersen

Title • Copenhagen from above

ISBN • 978-87-7900-694-2

1st edition, 2nd printing

Text • Claus Hagen Petersen
Photos • Henrik Schurmann
Layout • Henrik Schurmann, Per Schou
Editor • Elin Holst
Publishers • Forlaget Globe
Translation • Dorte Holst

www.globe.dk

Book website: www.globe.dk/kobenhavn
Copyright © 2008 Forlaget Globe

Pictures on pages 90-91:
The Little Mermaid
© Edvard Eriksen/billedkunst.dk

Pictures on pages 140-141:
The genetically modified paradise
© Bjørn Nørgaard/billedkunst.dk

Contents

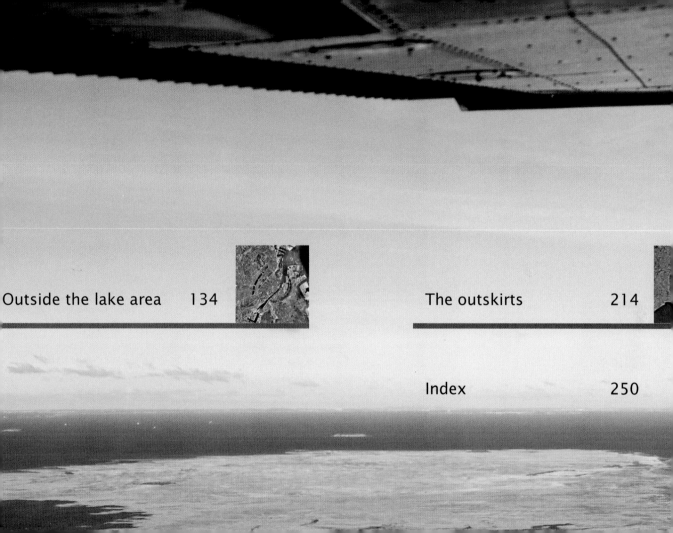

Preface

"Look at your city from the top of the tower" a Danish band once encouraged Copenhageners to do. A very Copenhagen-like way of doing things: taking the broad view – looking at things from a distance and allowing yourself to look at the city in a new way. Perhaps you can find the spot again where you met your first love or perhaps just make out your office somewhere. You can also enjoy the city's peculiar patterns and symmetry that you will never discover when walking the streets.

The publishers sent photographer Henrik Schurmann hunting under the clouds for Copenhagen's conspicuous characteristics. Together, we have selected over 200 of the thousands of photos he took. The photos, locations and history are supplemented with insight and understanding by Claus Hagen Petersen, whose precise comments provide the essentials without going into tedious and trivial detail.

With this book the publishers wish to pay tribute to the city and its people, places and sights in a subtle and fascinating manner. We hope that others will enjoy the book as much as we have enjoyed launching this great project and seeing the results of our efforts.
Thank you to Copenhagen and the Copenhageners for a great experience!

The structure of the book

We begin our tour of Copenhagen within the lake area above Slotsholmen and move towards the Medieval Town, Christianshavn and Frederiksstaden – in other words the areas that made up the "town of ramparts" until 1856. Then we continue above the area that lies like a braiding between the old rampart area and the lakes in the direction south-north.

In the section "Outside the lake area" we take the opposite direction. We pass the old residential area heading from Østerbro and Nørrebro, Frederiksberg and Vesterbro to end up in Sydhavnen and finally above Amager. You will find some significant places and locations further away at the end of the book under the heading "The outskirts".

Join us at Google Earth

Visit the book's website on www.globe.dk/kobenhavn that provides the coordinates for the pictures, allowing you to see the same motive from the same angle on Google Earth. You can navigate on your own to see more of the surroundings in detailed satellite photos. Google Earth is a free program for your computer. You can download it from Google's website: http://earth.google.com. This book's website also offers more pictures from Copenhagen and its surroundings.

Forlaget Globe

The author

Claus Hagen Petersen was born in 1949. He is a journalist and radio program host at P1 DR.
MA (history, social science, Danish). Long-term teacher.
Journalist, TV host at TV 2 1988-2001. "Here & Now (guest of the week) (1988-1996), "Københavns historie 1-6" (1996) and "Danmark i 1000 år 1-13" (1998-1999). TV host of Deadline DR 2 (2001-2003), radio program host at P1 DR "Ugen på spidsen" since 2004.
Author of several books, including "Sidste tur over Storebælt" (1998), "De 100 mest betydningsfulde danskere i det 20. århundrede" (with Connie Hedegaard) (1999) and "Politikens bog om København" (2004).
Lecturer and guide on tours of the Copenhagen harbour and canals.

The photographer

Henrik Schurmann, photographer, author and PhD (biology). Worked for ten years as a researcher at Danish universities. For the past eight years, he has been occupied with authoring, journalism and photography. Henrik is the author of more than 15 books on photography and image editing. His latest book is about digital mirror reflection photography. As a photographer, he is especially interested in capturing the detail, preferably from an unusual angle.

Within the lake area

The island of Slotsholmen

The entire Medieval Town and more. If we had been able to fly 800 years ago, we would have seen Absalon's small white fortress where we now see the tower of Christiansborg Palace.

On Bremerholm, on the opposite side of what is today a canal, we would find the beginnings of the naval harbour, which was later to become Gammelholm. The fortress and the fleet protected the small town that emerged at Gammel Strand, and which was provided towards land with a system of ramparts that constituted the borders of Copenhagen for 500 years.

Fragments of the system of ramparts can be seen in the green areas of Tivoli (left) and the H. C. Ørsted park (in the middle). To the north, the rampart ran along the present street of Gothersgade on the inner side of the Kongens Have park (right).

This was the size of the Medieval Town. It could easily fit under the Great Belt bridge.

Today, Slotsholmen is surrounded by canals on three sides. In medieval times it was an island (by the fortress) in the sea opposite Zealand, about a third of its present size. Most of what we know today as Slotsholmen has been filled up. This is also true of the other areas in the lower third of the picture. In the Middle Ages, this was open sea.

Christiansborg Palace

This has been the centre of power for more than 800 years. Our focus is on Christiansborg Palace on Slotsholmen. Christian VI decided to have the old Copenhagen Palace demolished and to build a magnificent palace instead in accordance with the despot's self-understanding.

The first Christiansborg Palace was constructed from 1733 to 1740, but burned down as early as in 1794, the flames leaving only the buildings surrounding the riding ground. Bad things comes in threes as the saying goes, and in quick succession followed the bombardment of Copenhagen, the state bankruptcy and the loss of Norway. All this meant that it took more than 30 years to build a new palace. The second Christiansborg Palace was completed in 1828. This was where Frederik VII abolished despotism in 1848, and where the constitutional assembly held its meetings. This palace burned in 1884 except for the palace church (bottom right) with its characteristic colonnade entrance; an example of C. F. Hansen's New Classicism style that was trend-setting at the beginning of the 19th century.

The site of the fire was left unused for many years until the building of a third palace started in 1907 with the architect Thorvald Jørgensen in charge. During the digging for the foundations, the remains of Absalon's fortress and Copenhagen's old palace were discovered. It is still possible to see the ruins in the basement; the entry is in the central main gate in the palace courtyard.

The palace is Denmark's first major concrete building, covered with stones gathered from all parts of the country. The ground plan has the shape of a U where the right leg (towards the canal in the picture) was intended for the king as living quarters and the left for the people, holding the two chambers of Parliament (Folketinget and Landstinget). But Christian X did not wish to move in, he preferred to stay at Amalienborg; the right decision everyone agrees today. However, the royal family does use the great hall for large gala events.

Folketinget, which had been rehoused elsewhere, returned to the new Christiansborg in 1918. The parliament hall is behind the large first-floor windows to the left in the building facing on the palace courtyard.

Det Kongelige Bibliotek
– The Royal Library

The garden at the Royal Library is the only green oasis on Slotsholmen.

Originally, it was laid out as a naval harbour in the earliest years of Christian IV's government! Here, the navy's ships were provided with powder and ammunition from Tøjhuset (left) and with provisions from Provianthuset (right). You can still see heavy mooring rings in the garden and thus be reminded of the history of the area.

The long building at the top of the picture still contains Rigsarkivet (the Public Records). Frederik III set up his cabinet of curiosities in the new building in the 1660s, and in 1673 he installed his private book collection on the first floor.

This was the start of the Royal Library, which was opened to the public in 1793. In 1849, it became state property.

In 1906, the library moved to a new building designed by H. J. Holm.

The main entrance faces the library garden and cannot be seen. However, we can see the tops of the two towers flanking the entrance. In 1968, an office building was added; it is now covered and thus cannot be seen.

In 1999, a new chapter was written in the history of the library. It moved to the new building, Den Sorte Diamant (the black diamond). The building inclines threateningly over the harbour, unorthodox with its skew lines and large glass area on the front side that throws light into the big central hall and further into the library rooms at the sides. The black stones come from Zimbabwe. The diamond sparkles most impressively from the harbour or from Christianshavn. Certainly not from the air.

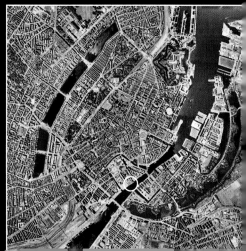

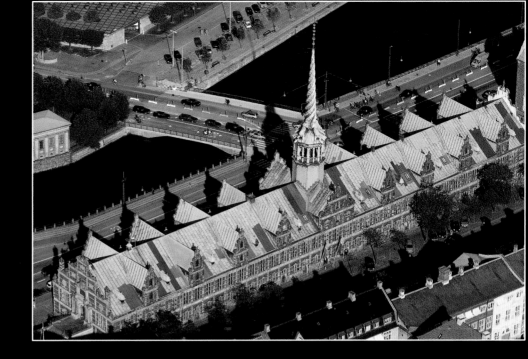

Børsen – commodity and stock exchange

Børsen's coiling dragon spire is one of the most well-known and characteristic elements in the Copenhagen skyline. It is made of wood and was mounted in 1625 when Christian IV's commodity exchange building had almost been completed. The spire was renewed in 1777.

Børsen was placed on a tongue in the harbour surrounded by water on three sides.

Thus, ships would unload and load on both sides of the building. Originally, the building was a commodity exchange boasting Copenhagen's first indoor shops (stalls) at street level. In the 19th century, the Copenhagen merchants gradually took over the building, and in 1857 the merchants' guild bought the building. The same year the building was scheduled as a monument – the first in the country. Today, the building houses the headquarters of the chamber of commerce.

Børsen is one of Copenhagen's oldest buildings and a grand example of Dutch Renaissance architecture, which characterized most of Christian IV's buildings.

Strøget

– Copenhagen's main pedestrian street

A look towards north east at the major part of the Medieval Town (and more). The name is somewhat misleading since scarcely any buildings from the Middle Ages exist any more. Several extensive fires have made sure of that.

But the streets still have the same crooked course that they have had for hundreds of years. This picture gives us a good impression of this.

At the bottom of the picture (a little to the right) you see people passing Gammeltorv square on their way to Nygade (new street), which is not that old. It is a result of a street breakthrough in 1691. Earlier it had been necessary to walk through the streets of Skindergade and Skoubogade to get to Vimmelskaftet. The name originates from a medieval, twisted hammer drill and came to be used as the name for the part of Strøget that crosses to the east (right). Vimmelskaftet takes us to Amagertorv square, which opens as a funnel. Here, generations of peasants from Amager offered their agricultural products for sale.

From Amagertorv, Østergade takes us towards Kgs. Nytorv. This street has always been the grandest in Copenhagen. It was the first street to be covered with flagstones, and traditionally, it is the home of the most exclusive shops with matching prices. In the last part of the street, they do not even put prices on the offerings. Not that this makes them any cheaper. The street names are another remnant from the Middle Ages. But not Strøget. Well into the 19th century, the Copenhageners' preferred promenade was called "the Route". The name of Strøget was launched in a summer revue in the 1880s and was only included on the street signs about 15 years ago.

Vor Frue Kirke

Copenhagen's cathedral

This was the target of the English bombard-ment in September 1807, that is, the spire of the then huge Baroque cathedral. The spire measuring more than one hundred meters fell down, crushing the church in a sea of flames.

So it was decided to erect a completely new cathedral in the New Classicism style of the time with C. F. Hansen in charge. The very chaste church is clearly inspired by that period's passion for antiquity, which is especially dominant in the front part facing Nørregade. The brown, plastered walls are no match for car fumes, which now and then give the church a somewhat depres-sing appearance. The rebuilding of Copenhagen's cathedral, which is the main church in Denmark, was completed in 1828.

There has been a church at this highest point of the Medieval town since the 13th century. The church was the Catholic church's main bastion, and in 1479 when Christian I obtained the pope's permission to establish Denmark's first university, it was placed right opposite the cathedral. The main building of the university (1836) still flanks Frue Plads square in the shadows of the cathedral. In the university courtyard you can see the building housing the governing body (with the embattled gable to the far left), which is one of just three buildings from the Middle Ages still left in Copenhagen.

The church's Catholic canons lived in the street of St. Kannikestræde, leading from Frue Plads square towards the Round Tower (at the top of the picture).

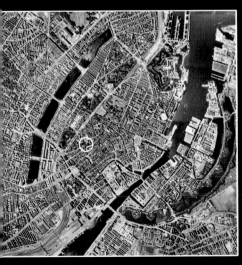

Gammeltorv and Nytorv squares

There are two squares. Gammeltorv (bottom) was the town's undisputed centre until Kgs. Nytorv was established at the end of the 17th century. From here, Vestergade (right edge, middle) and Nørregade (bottom middle) led to Vesterport and Nørreport, and this was the natural place for the town hall.

The ground plan of the town hall is clearly set off, and its position can be seen as a light square in the middle of the large square. Behind the town hall, an area gradually opened up to become a new square: Nytorv. The town hall burned to the ground in the great fire of 1795, and since it had been too small for many years, it was decided to build a completely new, much larger and combined court house and town hall.

C. F. Hansen's imposing town hall was placed at the upper corner of Nytorv. Here, the city's government was to be found for a hundred years. The building still houses Copenhagen's city court (at the top of the picture).

After the fire, Gammeltorv and Nytorv were joined into the oblong square we know today. Gammeltorv boasts the Caritas fountain, which is actually Denmark's only remaining street well from the Renaissance. It was provided with water from Emdrup lake via a complex piping system. On the majesty's birthday, golden apples balance on the fountain's water columns.

Nytorv features a more macabre piece of street furniture': the platform under the white lorry indicates the city's scaffold – a platform for public execution or punishment!

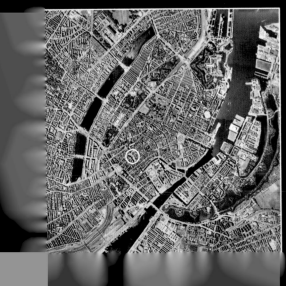

It is one of Denmark's most well-known buildings. Rundetårn was part of a trinity (trinitatis) with a new university church, an observatory and a university library. Most Danes – and a fair amount of tourists – have climbed the 209 metres of twisting archway to have a look at the Medieval Town from a height of 36 metres. Christian IV wished to further astronomic studies in Tycho Brahe's spirit. The university observatory was situated at the top of the tower until 1861 when it was moved to Østervold.

The present public observatory opened in 1929. The Trinitatis Church and the Round Tower were Christian IV's last big project. He lived to see the completion of the tower in 1642, but not the church, which was inaugurated in 1656. For more than 200 years, the loft of the Trinitatis Church contained the university library; today it is used for exhibitions.

Visitors look down at the harbour with the spires of the churches of Nikolaj Kirke and Vor Frelser Kirke on Christianshavn catching their eye.

Knippelsbro bridge

The first simple wooden bridge between Slotsholmen and the new quarter of Christianshavn was built 1618-20. The bridge was named after the first bridge-master, Hans Knip.

The present bridge was inaugurated in 1937 and has been conveying the ever increasing traffic for more than 70 years. It is a high-level bridge that starts with a ramp opposite the old Børsen building (left), raising in its passage of Privat-banken's old headquarters to reach the actual bridge with the characteristic towers, which were built at Burmeister & Wain.

Having made it to Christianhavn, we come into the street of Torvegade with the Foreign Ministry's large complex at the top of the harbour and Burmeister & Wain's old headquarters, built in 1962 and now taken over by the Nordea banking group.

The spire of Vor Frelser Kirke
– Our Saviour's Church

The fantastic corkscrew spire is literally winding 86 metres skywards and is not just the landmark of Christianshavn, but also one of the most characteristic elements in the city's skyline.

The exterior staircase winds four times around the copper clad spire before the bold climber makes it to the gilded sphere that supports Our Saviour's feet.

The spire was built in 1749-50 and was designed by Lauritz de Thurau. It steals the picture completely from the beautiful baroque church, which was inaugurated in 1696, and is one of Copenhagen's largest churches. Young people also enjoy the fantastic view towards Havnegade, and when they turn to the right, they get an equally magnificent view of the northern part of Christianshavn and Holmen.

Christianshavns Kanal

Christianshavn's canal was intended to be the high street of the new part of town that was built on poles in the sea opposite Copenhagen's harbour, at Christian IV's initiative.

The area was opened for development in 1618, but due to the

Touring the canals

Every summer, more than half a million people enjoy the harbour from the canal tour boats. A number that increases by 10% a year.

This makes the harbour tours one of the city's major attractions. It dates back to the 1920s when the tour ran from Børsen to the Little Mermaid and back. Today, Canal Tours and the competitor Nettobådene offer a number of tours that also include small trips to Frihavnen (Free Port) following a route on the other side of Holmen and Frederiksholms Kanal, possibly combined with a longer excursion to Sydhavnen and definitely passing Christianshavns Kanal (photo left).

The photographer is on the bridge leading from Sankt Annægade over the canal, capturing the harbour tour boat that sails through the entire canal from north to south. About 10 years ago, it was like sailing through a forest. An avenue of elm trees had to be felled due to Dutch elm disease. However, the canal area reappeared as an open urban space where the interaction between the old buildings and the canal setting became much more pronounced.

The free town of Christiania

The central part of Christiania where the reputed and infamous Pusher street runs hidden behind trees from the lower left corner, along the yellow building and further to the right, touching the yellow and grey end wall.

The Danish National Museum acquired one of the street's hash booths before the police removed these peculiar pieces of street furniture.

The yellow house in the street contains "Operaen" and Café Oasen. In the long house in the middle of the picture to the right at the foot of the chimney we find the pub called "Månefiskeren", whereas the inscription "Laboratoriebygningen" next to Christian IX's monogram above the entrance to the big red house at the top of the picture shows us the building's original use. The barracks in Rådmandsstræde opened in 1836 and served as barracks until 1970. The following year, the fence was smashed by activists, and all kinds of people began to move in. The free town of Christiania has existed for more than 35 years and a fair share of its residents are nearing retirement age; and perhaps the free town itself. Contrary to many earlier renewal projects, current plans to renew the area seem to be close to realisation. In some ways a pity.

The Free Town has been called a social experiment. You could add, for good or bad. On a beautiful summer's day, street life unfolds in rich nuances, supplemented by representatives from numerous ethnic minorities in the picturesque setting. On a drab winter's day, the impression of social misery for part of the Free Town's residents is reinforced and is very much displayed by some of its guests in the shadows of the worn-out buildings. And in public at that. Christiania comes third on the list of Copenhagen's tourist attractions!

The harbour with the Opera

The central part of the harbour in wide-screen. 50 years ago we would have seen the naval harbour at Holmen (to the right in the harbour) filled with warships, a crowd of cargo ships on their way to and from the southern part of the harbour Sydhavnen and a wealth of passenger ships at the quays at Kvæsthusbroen and Larsens Plads.

Now, all that is left is a single wooden ship at Larsens Plads, the harbour bus at the Opera, and at the bottom of the picture a small pleasure boat is braving the waves on its way through the harbour.

In return, cultural activities have taken over the scene. For decades, there were discussions about the building and position of a new theatre. Plans and projects were produced, but nothing happened. In 2000, shipowner Mærsk McKinney Møller offered to pay for a brand-new opera house on the condition that it was placed on Dokøen right opposite Amalienborg in continuation of the axis of Frederiksgade (see pages 68-69 and 72-73). Opinions of the architectural values of the opera house differ, but one thing is certainly true: it is difficult not to spot it at its central position in the harbour on the naval dockyard's old site.

Whether it was the private efficiency that woke up the public authorities we will never know. But the building of a new playhouse was finally initiated, and it can be seen under construction at Kvæsthusbroen to the left in the picture. At the bottom of the picture is a third cultural institution. The old Greenland warehouse today houses the cultural centre Nordatlantens Brygge.

The Opera by night

The 1450 windows sparkle like gold under the dark evening sky. A performance is on at the new opera house. The huge canopy protects the guests against rain when they finally reach their destination. The opera does have a central position in the harbour, but on the wrong side for most people.

The royal family can cross the harbour in their boat, but car people must take the long way around Christianshavn and Holmen in order to enjoy the performance.

Designed by architect Henning Larsen, the opera house was inaugurated in January 2005. By that time, 61,600 tonnes of cement had been used and the 4,900 square metres of wall surface were covered with 11,267 jura yellow limestone bricks from southern Germany.

The roof is 158 metres long and 90 metres wide, and the building, which is one of the largest in Denmark, has a floorage of 41,000 square metres. It is widely agreed that the building looks better on the inside than on the outside.

The difficult accessibility has given rise to an intense debate about footbridges and/or tunnels above/below the harbour; plans that are still only ideas.

With the Opera, Copenhagen has been given a new landmark.

The playhouse

The Royal Theatre has been wishing for a new playhouse for more than 100 years. The 1880s saw the breakthrough of modern naturalistic theatre, and the old stage of the Royal Theatre could not meet the physical requirements for closer contact to the audience that the intimate speech technique required.

An extension in the 1930s with a new stage was never any great success, and in the past decades, the Theatre has therefore been using a number of small theatres around Copenhagen, for instance Turbinehallerne.

In 2008, the acting activities will be gathered under the same roof in the new playhouse at Kvæsthusbroen, which extends over the harbour. The house is designed by architects Boje Lundgaard and Lene Tranberg. It contains three stages: the large main stage with 650 seats, a smaller gate stage with 200 seats and a small intimate stage with about 100 seats.

The playhouse has a floorage of 20,000 square metres and is thus half the size of its big brother on the other side of the harbour. The big gate tower is copper clad and gives you the impression of the superstructure of an ocean liner at quay.

Nyhavn and the Kongens Nytorv square

The area of the town had almost doubled when in the middle of the 17th century, the old rampart running along Gothersgade was relocated with direction towards the new fortress Kastellet. In the middle of the new large town, the king wished to establish a new magnificent square. The king's new square started to materialise in 1670, and of course the square had to have access to the harbour. From 1671-73 the new harbour or rather the new canal was dug: Nyhavn.

There has always been a big difference between the two sides of Nyhavn. On 'the nice side' (to the left in the big picture) we find Charlottenborg facing Kongens Nytorv. The mansion was named after Christian V' dowager queen Charlotte Amalie, who lived here from 1700 to 1714.

The Royal Academy of Fine Arts has occupied this building since its establishment in 1754.

Behind Charlottenborg (below in the picture) we find the large exhibition building that most people probably associate with Charlottenborg. It was built 1880-83. For many years, the entire area from Charlottenborg to the harbour was a large park that contained the Botanical Garden from 1778 to 1874.

55°40'33.76"N   12°34'48.52"E

Nyhavn
– the New Harbour

From the start, Nyhavn was too narrow and too shallow to be any great success as a harbour.

It was, however, used for long periods of time by the many small packet boats carrying packages and small general goods to the Danish islands and provincial harbours.

"The naughty side" developed into one of the most notorious parts of town with lots of murky sailors' joints with singing, sounds of drinking, whores, thieves and all kinds of tricksters as permanent elements.

But it was also the place where Danish Dixieland jazz and rock & roll music started at the end of the 1950s.

Today, the quay area has become an exclusive restaurant area that stretches as a single, endless bar from Kongens Nytorv to the harbour. On the quay, people sit drinking beer from the local grocer. The price level is somewhat different under the restaurants' white parasols.

ce-skating at Kongens Nytorv

ummer and winter at Kongens Nytorv. The magnificent square of espotism has a somewhat awkward form that did not quite natch baroque requirements for order and symmetry. The estab-shment of Krinsen was to remedy this. Abraham Lamoureux's equestrian statue of Christian V symbolises early despotism's elf-understanding. Before the age of television and weekly nagazines, grateful subjects had to experience the majesty in the orm of a statue.

But they could admire him from all angles on the promenade hat was established as a circle round the "horse" after its nauguration in 1688. Krinsen was removed in 1749, re-stablished partly in 1860 and fully in 1916. The statue was retired

in 1946 when it was rather worn and one leg was sagging. It was replaced with the present copy.

The character of Krinsen and the entire square changed completely in 1998 when the old sick elm trees had to go. New trees have been planted (this time limes), and in 1999 the splendid idea of establishing an ice-skating rink in wintertime on Krinsen was realised as part of the revitalisation of the proud square that suffers badly because of the heavy car traffic.

So now ice skaters can wonder about despotism and its magnificence while circling the statue that Copenhagen youngsters have been celebrating for generations when having passed their upper secondary exams.

55°40'49.87"N 12°35'9.42"E

Magasin

The building has a special kind of nostalgic modernity. The illuminated windows are in contrast to the heavy building and send a signal to those passing by on Kongens Nytorv about life and enjoyment. Here, your dreams can be fulfilled, if you have the money, that is.

Two enterprising merchants, Theodor Wessel and Emil Vett, joined forces and opened a draper's shop in Aarhus in 1868. As true entrepreneurs they expanded their business with shops all over Denmark. The Copenhagen branch was established in rented premises at the then Hotel du Nord, which they gradually took over. The fine old hotel was demolished in 1893/94 and replaced by the present building. Part of the name survived since the

partners registered the company name Magasin du Nord in 1879. The Magasin building is one example of Copenhagen's ambition 110 years ago to become a metropolis.

A modern department store in a monumental building of Parisian appearance with porters in uniform, glass lifts and a selection of everything your heart could desire was a natural part of a metropolis. Most people saw a visit to Magasin as something special, an expression of a life style long before this concept was invented.

Many other department stores came and went in step with the changes in consumption patterns. But Magasin keeps sparkling at night on Kongens Nytorv, even though the company has been through some hard times during the past decade.

Mainly in the Winter Room behind the ground-floor windows to the west (left). Or in the adjoining offices and private apartments. All rooms have intact interiors, and a visit gives you a genuine renaissance experience.

Rosenborg is the town's castle of the 17th century. Frederik IV considered it old-fashioned and built his own pleasure palaces (Frederiksberg, Fredensborg) and then the royal family almost stopped using the castle. Rosenborg Castle, which was provided with electric light only a few years ago, today contains the crown jewels and the crown regalia and a museum for the Oldenburg family from Christian IV to the last Oldenburger, Frederik VII.

Rose garden and playground

Kongens Have park or Rosenborg Have was laid out as a renaissance garden in connection with the building of Rosenborg Castle.

As the town's oldest park it has been through different periods' varying ideas of what gardens should look like and what they should express. Today, the garden thus contains elements from the original renaissance garden, but baroque times' demand for order and symmetry also has influence, contrasting the features of a 19th-century, English landscape garden.

When we look at it all from above, we can see that the garden's history is taken into account in connection with new additions. The rose garden (left) and the playground completely fulfil the baroque demand for symmetry and accuracy. The playground (opposite page) has its architectural basis in the myth about the dragon, the golden sphere (at the centre) and the four kingdoms.

Domes and stars

A grand northward view of a large part of New Copenhagen. The designation New Copenhagen is to be seen in contrast to the Medieval Town.

In connection with the reorganisation of the ramparts in the middle of the 17th century, the area of the town was doubled, with the entire area between Kongens Nytorv and Kastellet being included in the town.

New Copenhagen consists of the posh Frederiksstaden, which takes up most of the picture, but also the more modest quarters of Borgergade and Adelgade to the far left. Paradoxically, it is here that we find the largest concentration of old buildings anywhere in Copenhagen. The reason is that this area has never been victim to the big town fires.

In the middle of the picture, the posh street Bredgade extends towards Kastellet. The Marmorkirken church adds its characteristic outline to the city's skyline, and Amalienborg Castle is in every way the natural centre of Frederiksstaden. To the

north at Toldboden, the A. P. Møller-Mærsk shipping group has its headquarters under the seven-pointed star in the modern white office buildings. At the top of the picture, you can see Frihavnen and Langelinie, with a visiting cruise liner and a naval ship.

At the opposite side of the harbour is Refshaleøen, for decades the domicile of the Burmeister & Wain shipyard. Further into the harbour, the museum frigate Peder Skram is safely anchored across the harbour at the Elefantmolen pier.

as the absolute gem. It was to this mansion that Christian VII moved after the fire at Christiansborg Palace in 1794.

The wooden colonnade takes us to Schack's mansion (Christian IX's mansion). This building has provided residential quarters for Frederik VI, Christian IX and now Queen Margrethe. The regent is not at home since the flag does not fly from the flagpole. We continue counter-clockwise to Brockdorff's mansion (Frederik VIII's mansion).

Here, Frederik VIII and Frederik IX had their residences. The building is currently (2007) being renovated to allow Crown Prince Frederik to move in with his family. We stop at the upper left corner where we find Levetzau's mansion (Christian VIII's mansion). It was the residence of Christian VIII and Christian X. The ground floor contains the Amalienborg museum in which there is public access to the latest four kings' workrooms.

On the high horse

The French sculptor Francois Saly worked on the statue for 21 years. But it took only three minutes to cast the statue in Gjethuset at Kongens Nytorv. Two hundred soldiers then spent two days pulling the construction from Kongens Nytorv to Amalienborg. The equestrian statue of Frederik V was unveiled in 1771, but by then the king had been long gone.

The statue was placed at the centre of the square where the two axes cross (pages 68-69). The Frederiksgade axis starts at Marmorkirken (large picture) that Frederik V is looking at (even though it

was not completed until much later) (see pages 76-77). King and church were the social pillars of despotic Denmark.

Now, the axis of power ends with the opera house at Dokøen (medium-sized picture seen in the opposite direction). Church, king and culture, or some might say church, king and financial power are lined up like pearls on a string.

Frederik V has a strongly idealised expression like a Roman emperor with a laurel wreath, masterfully towering above everybody and everything in the kingdom.

The park at the castle

The Amaliehaven park lies between Amalienborg castle and the part of the harbour that was previously called Larsens Plads.

The park was created by the Belgian architect Jean Delogne. It was inaugurated in 1983 following a heated public debate. It is not a particularly popular park – rather a modern baroque park with order and symmetry.

The closeness to Amalienborg castle provides a somewhat solemn atmosphere, and the park does not invite sunbathing or beer drinking. There is a grand view of the harbour (outside the bottom picture) towards Amalienborg's square. The impressive fountain is on the Frederiksgade axis that starts at Marmorkirken and continues directly through the equestrian statue and the fountain to end in the Opera at the opposite side of the harbour.

Marmorkirken – the marble church

It is called Frederikskirken, but its name was to have been Frederik's Danish Church when Frederik V laid the foundation stone in 1749. The work commenced based on plans prepared by the chief architect for this part of town, Nicolai Eigtved. After Eigtved's death, the construction was taken over by French N. H. Jardin, who worked based on his own strongly revised drawings. In 1770, the building had reached a height of 20 metres, and then the work was stopped by J. F. Struense. The site remained a picturesque ruin for more than 100 years (!), frequently used by artists as a Greek-style setting, until the industrial magnate C. F. Tietgen bought the site and completed the building project.

The church was inaugurated in 1894.

The church is covered with Norwegian marble.

Eighteen Fathers of the Church, made 1884-1887, stand on the balustrade 20 metres above street level. The impressive dome is crowned by a lantern at a height of 60 metres.

Behind the lantern, you can see the court of Østre Landsret on the corner of the streets of Bredgade and Fredericiagade.

The building was erected as an opera house, has contained the naval college and has been used as barracks. After the fire at Christiansborg Palace in 1884, parliament was rehoused in the building. It was here that the constitution was passed in 1915. The parliament moved back to the new Christiansborg in 1918. The three gilded domes are part of the Alexander Nevsky church in Bredgade. The Russian church was built 1881-83, and the construction work was followed closely by Russian Tsar Alexander and his Danish wife Dagmar.

At the end of the street of Bredgade, which crosses the picture from the lower right corner, we find the mansions of Dehn and Bernstorff – two of the city's grandest private mansions.

Gefion

The goddess Gefion is looking down Amaliegade from her place at the entrance to Langelinie. She is in total control of the team of oxen pulling the big plough.

The myth talks about the Swedish king Gylfe who offered Gefion as much land as she could plough in a day and a night with her four sons pulling the plough. They were turned into oxen for the occasion, and Gefion ploughed an area in Sweden that was placed in the sea between Funen and Scania. This was the origin of Zealand, and the hole in Sweden became the lake Mäleren.

The Gefion fountain is the city's largest monument. It was made by the sculptor Anders Bundgaard and was inaugurated in 1908.

Star shape

Just imagine if the Swedes were to return. They had taken the capital by storm in 1659, and Denmark's existence had hung by a thread. The result was bad enough. The Danish provinces east of Øresund had been lost; forever as it turned out.

Copenhagen had become a border town, and in case the Swedes were to reappear, it was necessary to reinforce the town's fortifications. The Dutch fortification engineer Henrik Rüse (later ennobled as Rysensteen) was called in, and he was the prime mover in the construction of the Kastellet fortress, which was erected in record time (1661-1664).

The fortress was built according to the strict baroque requirements for symmetry, which we can see when we look at the entire complex from the air. The ramparts have the shape of a pentagon with five characteristic bastions pointing in different directions. It has now become possible once more to walk on all the ramparts after an old railway track that ran from the railway terrain around Østerport to Toldboden, has been removed. This has enabled Copenhageners to take up the old tradition of walking on the ramparts on the evening before Common Prayer Day.

Kastellet was also an expression of early despotism's self-understanding and a signal to the people, telling them who was in charge.

Thus, the ramparts and the guns also pointed towards Copenhagen from the completely closed fortress! In the foreground, the King's gate leads us into Kastellet. Right behind the gate is the main guard, and the military intelligence is quartered in the old red blocks. At the top, the Norwegian gate serves as a back door to the old fortress.

Copenhagen on foot

The first walkathon was held in 1999. It was the shoe manufacturer Ecco that got the splendid idea of combining exercise with fund-raising. Your feet donate money and your eyes gather impressions. You can choose between two routes of 6 and 10 kilometres, respectively, that take the participants through historic surroundings. Each kilometre that the individual participant covers means five Danish kroner for charity. The walk starts and ends at Kastellet. Crowds and queuing are common when the many thousand participants are to pass through the narrow gate on their way into Copenhagen.

The idea has spread to all parts of the world, and an estimate says that about 200,000 people have donated money while exercising since the first steps were taken in 1999.

Nyboder and Østerport

We are in the same place in the air space as on pages 80-81, but the photographer has turned the camera a little to the west. Thus, we find Kastellet to the right in the picture, and in the middle Østerport Station and the large railway terrain that runs along Frihavnen. The old Østerport gate was situated just about where the station is now, and it was the town's gateway to the north until 1856. Part of the old ramparts is still preserved in the Østre Anlæg park that you can see stretching from the middle of the picture as a green wedge to the left border.

Inside the ramparts, Nyboder's yellow blocks make a bright sight. The boatswains' blocks were built on what was then the northernmost area behind the town ramparts. Christian IV wanted to build a whole town quarter for the fleet's permanent staff, and the first block was completed in 1631. Only a single house from Christian IV's time has been preserved; it is the yellow building in the bottom left corner close to St. Paul's church.

Nyboder was extended several times during the 18th century, all the way up to Østerport. In the 19th century, many of the old blocks were demolished to make room for dreary barracks (bottom left corner).

Nyboder was a state within the town with its own rules and police. Even today you have to have a connection with the navy in order to be able to live in the old boatswains' blocks, which are more idyllic to look at than practical to live in. In many ways, this building project was ahead of its time, applying the principles of modern terraced houses, as you can see on the next pages.

Langelinie

The area known as Langelinie consists of several elements.

To the south is the park that starts at Toldboden and continues on the outside of Kastellet to the Little Mermaid and the large marina. Then there is the Langelinie quay that marks the harbour front to the north, on the eastern side of Frihavnen. The park contains many different sculptures. The impressive column has been erected in memory of the naval hero Ivar Huitfeld, who distinguished himself in a naval battle during the Great Northern War.

It was erected in 1886. The guns at the foot of the base were retrieved from the wreckage of his ship "Dannebroge" in the Køge Bugt bay.

In 2005, the Danish consul in Hiroshima, Selichi Takaki, gave the City of Copenhagen 200 Japanese cherry trees to celebrate the 200th year of H.C. Andersen's birth. In spring, all the buds adorn the park with a pink tinge. In both pictures, the Langeliniepavillonen restaurant can be seen, and in the upper picture, a little bit of Kastellet as well (to the left).

Small and popular

t can be difficult to fathom, but the modest sculpture on the beach at Lange-inie is probably what most people in this world associate with Denmark. The figure s donated by brewery owner Carl Jacobsen, who got the idea while attending the fairytale ballet "The Little Mermaid" at the Royal Theatre. She was created by the sculptor Edvard Eriksen and unveiled in 1913. The brewery-owner and the sculptor had many discussions during her creation about where she should be placed and whether she should have legs or a fishtail.

She has been sitting on her rock for about 100 years now, looking at the human beings that she so wished to be like. And she has been looking at quite a lot of people. An estimated 1 million say hello to Denmark's major sight every year, either from the shore or from the harbour tour boats. Many tourists wonder at how small she is.

She is only 1.25 metres tall, but her weight is 175 kilos! The Little Mermaid has been subjected to several attacks. Thus, her head was sawed off twice (1964, 1998). In both cases, the vandalism was investigated by the police in line with the most serious murder cases.

private rooms.

In front of the funnel is the engine and the crew's quarters. Dannebrog is managed by the queen's captain of the royal yacht, who is in charge of a crew of nine officers, seven sergeants and 36 conscripts.

Since 1932, the ship has covered more than 300,000 nautical miles.

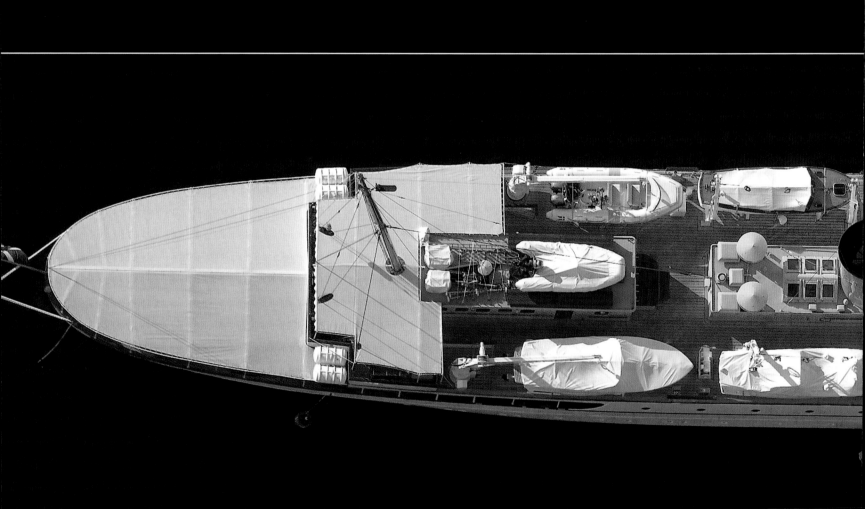

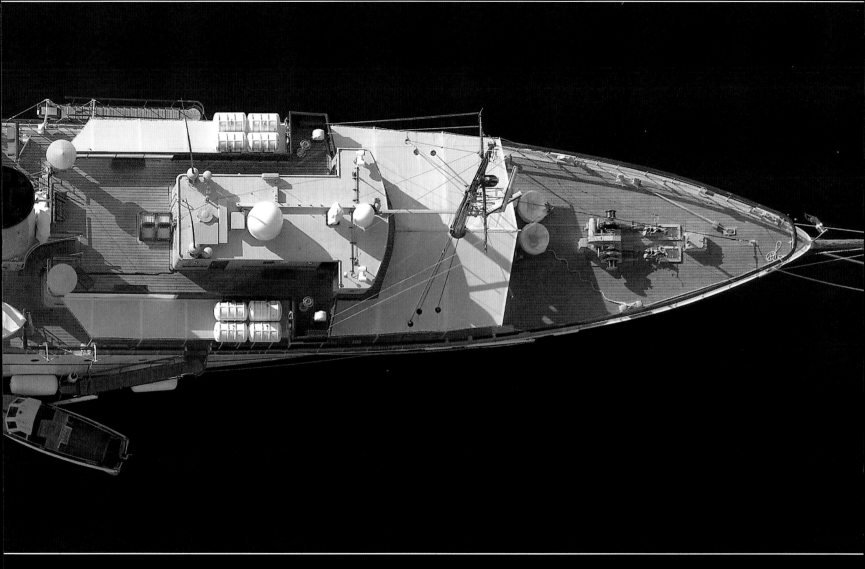

The Tre Kroner fort

It has marked the entrance to Copenhagen's harbour since 1776. First as a sea fort, later as a landmark.

The name comes from a previous sea fort, which was built on top of the hull of an old naval ship called Tre Kroner.

The sea fort has had a chequered career. When its role as protector of the entrance to the harbour ended, it served among other things as barracks and as a searchlight station. In the 1930s there was a cinema out here (!), and during the German occupation, the Germans provided the fort with anti-aircraft defences. After the war, the fort dilapidated, and the small horseshoe harbour was for many years used for dumping old ships.

Now, the old sea fort has once more been restored to its former glory. The harbour tour boats call on the fort, and you can see the dungeons and visit the cosy restaurant in the red building to the right of the entrance. But always remember to catch the last boat back!

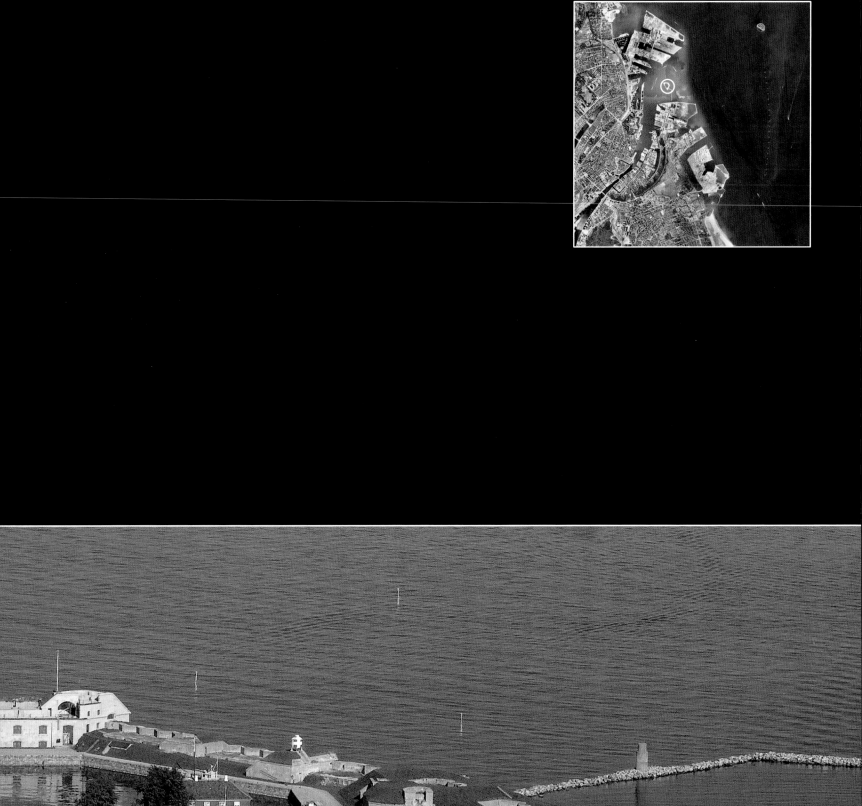

Holmen

Had we been in this place 400 years ago, all our eyes would have seen was the open sea. Practically everything we can see now is built on added material and poles hammered into the seabed.

Our view is south-north. Like a boomerang, Christianshavn's ramparts are winding through the picture from the lower left corner, encircling Christianshavn (at the bottom) and Holmen (in the middle of the picture).

At the top is Refshaleøen, for many years the domicile of Burmeister & Wain's shipyard. The huge mounting building is still there as a remnant from the shipyard that was for many years Denmark's largest workplace.

Space at Gammelholm (opposite Christiansborg Palace) had become scarce, and from the 1680s a new naval station was built in the sea. Initially, Nyholm was established in the north, and the work continued towards the south. At Nyholm (at the back), you can see the frigate "Peder Skram" lying at Elefantmolen perpendicular into the harbour. Further south we find Frederiksholm, which is the central island of Holmen. The old store houses and workshops have been turned into exciting flats, just as a number of institutions for creative education (the National Film School, the Rhythmic Music Conservatory and the School of Architecture) have moved out here. South of Frederiksholm is Arsenaløen. Somewhat isolated in the harbour, the Opera takes up most of Dokøen, which in naval times held the naval dockyard.

At the bottom of the picture (to the left) you can see the northern part of Christianshavn.

Gunboat houses and the rigging sheers

The picturesque gunboat houses at the eastern side of Frederiksholm were added after the bombardment of Copenhagen.

The English came for the Dano-Norwegian fleet, and they left with it following the bombardment and Copenhagen's surrender in 1807. As a poor replacement, a large number of small gunboats were built, and they were kept in new, shed-like buildings at Frederiksholm. For reasons unknown, the old wooden buildings survived, but were in a tumble-down state when the navy left Holmen in 1992. The picturesque setting with the fine sea view had a magnetic effect on small, trendy businesses, especially within advertising and the media world.

They have taken over the old gunboat houses; almost all of them have been completely renovated. A section burned one evening in 2006. Fortunately, there was no wind; otherwise things could have turned out really bad at Holmen.

At the top to the right on the opposite page we are at Nyholm. The old rigging sheers were built under Christian VI and obtained the status of the harbour's landmark. Through the years, many masts have been rigged at springtime on the navy's old sailboats. The submarine "Sælen" was the last active submarine in the navy's service. It is now placed at Nyholm, serving as a museum (bottom right on page 99).

A view of central Copenhagen

An overall view of central Copenhagen. The curved railway area sets a frame for the inner part of Vesterbro (bottom left). The brown and white buildings of the central meat market were established close to the railway to facilitate the transportation of animals for slaughter. North of Vesterbro on the other side of the lakes, Nørrebro and then Østerbro with the Svanemølleværket power station whose three tall chimneys can be noticed at the bay.

The green areas to the right in the picture are the remains of the old ramparts that formed a green iron ring around Copenhagen until 1856. Today, there are remnants of them in Tivoli and the parks of H. C. Ørstedsparken, the botanical garden and Østre Anlæg.

Copenhagen's first railway station was placed outside the ramparts, when the railway to Roskilde was inaugurated in 1847. The present station, which is the third, is located in the same place.

More than 100,000 people pass Denmark's largest station daily, and almost all Danes have at one point been in Heinrich Wenck's beautiful building from 1911 and boarded a train under the impressive wooden constructions above the 12 tracks (see pages 104-105).

Bottom right the Postal Terminal and in the corner, DSB's (Danish Railways) old goods terminal, which is to be the future domicile of Rigsarkivet (the public records).

The Planetarium

The Tycho Brahe Planetarium is located at the end of the lake of Skt. Jørgen where the City of Copenhagen previously stored road salt. For a time in the 1980s, the salt storehouse served as a venue for rhythmic music.

The Planetarium is a centre for popular astronomy. In addition to permanent exhibitions about astronomy and space research, the building contains a space theatre where 240 people at a time can experience space and 4000 stars by means of a star projector and an IMAX projector, which can also show advanced IMAX films and 3D films on the large, vaulted screen that measures 823 square metres. Designed by the architect Knud Munk, the Planetarium was inaugurated in 1989. The building has the form of a truncated cone, just about the same height as the Round Tower; it is made of yellow bricks decorated with blue, glazed patterns.

The Planetarium quickly became one of the city's major tourist attractions, welcoming one million visitors already in 1991.

Hoved-
banegården
- the central station

Hovedbanegården was inaugurated in 1911
as the third in a row. The main building
crosses the 12 tracks and consists of a
departure hall and an arrival hall, which has
now been joined into a single, large space
that is visited daily by more than 100,000
people. In 1917 Boulevardbanen started to
be used, and Hovedbanegården thus
became a through station. In this
connection, the huge pit was dug (on the
opposite side of the building towards
Vesterbrogade and the Liberty Memorial)
that ever since has been a subject for
discussion. The central station was
inaugurated in the railway's heyday where
stations were grand buildings that were to
enhance the cities' image. Here, strangers,
both Danes from the provinces and
foreigners, got their first impression of
Copenhagen, and from here,
Copenhageners bid the city farewell.

   Heinrich Wenck's station has for almost
100 years met changing requirements for
functionality, even though track space has
become scarce in recent years. The pulse is
the highest in the city, impacting the
surrounding quarters that have developed
into a real metropolitan area through the
years. In the upper right corner, Arne
Jacobsen's SAS hotel thus thrust its
towering contour into the air (1960). To
the left of the hotel you can see the big
white curved building and then
"Vesterport" with its green copper roof. At
the bottom of the picture you can see the
main post office.

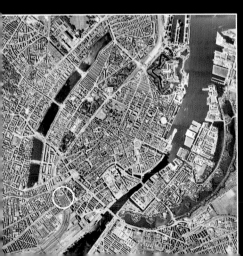

Tivoli's lights

The lights try to tempt people passing by to visit the illuminated garden. But it is difficult to do so on such a dark and cold April evening.

Tivoli's main entrance has been in the same place ever since the opening in 1843. The present stately main entrance is designed by the architects Emil Blichfeldt and Richard Bergmann (1889).

It was part of a major complex with the Apollo theatre and the Wivel restaurant (later Wivex), which both disappeared about 35 years ago.

More than 100,000 lamps illuminate the old garden, creating a fairytale atmosphere. The frigate in the lake seems to be exchanging shots (top left), the tower of the attraction "Himmelskibet" makes you think of a major rocket launch (top left), the trees at the lake are illuminated as if Copenhagen was once more being bombarded (middle) and the Chinese Tower appears more oriental than in daylight as it is reflected in the lake (top right). The lights have a special effect on dark December days where Tivoli in recent years has been open for Christmas.

Tivoli

When in 1843 Georg Carstensen was permitted to establish "Kjøbenhavns Tivoli og Vauxhall", the town was still a fortress encircled by ramparts and moats. The amusement park was therefore placed on the outside of Stadsgraven so that the Copenhageners had to pass the old Vesterport gate, which was located at the present townhall square (top left), when they were to entertain themselves in the garden and return in time before the gate was closed. Following the fall of the ramparts in 1856, the town exploded, and in a few years Tivoli was located in the middle of Copenhagen on a small part of the old

ramparts. Thus, the Tivoli lake is a remnant of the old moat.

The main entrance at Vesterbrogade (left) gives a hint of the axis that cuts through the garden, passing the Pantomime theatre (Tivoli's oldest building from 1874) and "Plænen", the large open space in the middle of the garden, to end in the large concert hall (right), which was inaugurated in 1956.

North of the axis, in the middle of the garden, you can see the layered roof of "Glassalen". In the upper left corner, the building of the Confederation of Danish Industries and the small miniature castle form the border of Tivoli opposite the town hall.

The castle has an uncertain future because there are plans for erecting a very tall building at this place. These plans have given rise to an extremely heated debate about tall buildings in inner Copenhagen.

Tivoli opens occasionally outside the traditional season. Thus, the Christmas market is about to become a permanent tradition, and the gates also open at other special occasions such as Halloween in October.

The world's highest merry-go-round

Some of the city's old towers and a completely new one. In 2006, Tivoli's new breakneck attraction "Himmelskibet" or the celestial ship opened, adding to city of towers' skyline.

With its 80 metres, Himmelskibet is the world's highest merry-go-round. The experience is said to be a mixture of horror, a classic merry-go-round ride combined with flying sensations and a fantastic view.

The twelve chairs, each with two seats, revolve at a speed of 70 kilometres an hour. The celestial aspect is emphasized by the decoration, which symbolises tools from the world of the astronomer Tycho Brahe, as you can at the top of the tower.

The photo cheats; the town hall tower is actually 25 metres higher than "Himmelskibet". To the extreme left is the spire of the church of St. Petri and at the bottom to the right is the main post office.

Business and pleasure

Serious politics influence the work at the town hall (top right), whereas the challenges of globalization and competitiveness are being pondered on the opposite side of H. C. Andersens Boulevard. The complex delimits Tivoli towards the street of Vesterbrogade.

Himmelskibet has been erected close to Tivoli's concert hall to the left in the picture, and it is easy to sense the axis from the concert hall towards the large stage at the opposite end of the "Plænen" area. Traditionally, the most noisy attractions have been placed in the area along the street of Tietgensgade. The new rollercoaster is no exception. The by-far most noisy attraction in the history of Tivoli has led to complaints from the cultural solemnity at the Glyptotek just opposite the garden. At the bottom, the police headquarters symbolises another kind of solemnity.

The Glyptotek museum

Brewery owner Carl Jacobsen wished to give his private art collection to the public if the City of Copenhagen would contribute a building site. Vilhelm Dahlerup's main building, with a strong element of renaissance in its architectural expression, was finished in 1897.

The enormous dome covers a winter garden at the centre of the museum, placed amidst all the cultural elements. From the winter garden the visitor is led into the large building behind, which was designed by Hack Kampmann and built 1901-06, to a kind of indoor Roman square (forum) flanked with columns and busts.

The art objects from Antiquity form the core of Ny Carlsbergs Glyptotek's extensive collections that also include an abundant selection of Danish and French art from the past 200 years.

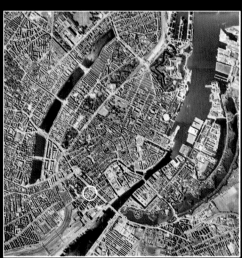

Police headquarters

The building symbolises power to such a degree that it is almost fascist in its expression. The police headquarters is from the time when the administration of justice was reformed and the executive power and the judicial power were clearly separated, also when it came to addresses and domiciles. Therefore, the Copenhagen police was to have new headquarters on the last big available site in the Rysensteen quarter.

Hack Kampmann designed the project, which commenced in 1918 and was completed in 1924. The irregular shape of the building site determined the ground plan of the building, which is almost triangular, but with an obtuse corner at the bottom of the picture. This is where we find the main entrance to the 'yard'. From here we enter the large circular 1615 sq. metres courtyard that is encircled by 44 double columns.

With its classical expression it seems to be inspired by the Pantheon in Rome and its 44 metres diameter has a similar size. Two circular corridors lead around the courtyard on the first and second floors, making it a confusing experience for strangers to find their way round the building.

The monumental complex is one of the last major new classicist buildings to have been built in Northern Europe. Its monumental appearance is emphasized by the fact that the windows in the gloomy facades open only inwards. It would not do to be in any way unrestrained.

Town hall

Powerful in its appearance, with respect for Danish architectural traditions and with a wealth of detail outside and inside. Martin Nyrup was the man behind the town's house, which was built from 1895 to 1905 on the old ramparts. The old town hall on the Nytorv square had become too small (you can see the back of this at the top to the left).

The new town hall was a manifest to the modern city's self-understanding as expressed in the imposing tower that stands 105.6 metres tall. There is public access to the balcony at a height of 60 metres (right below the clock), which offers an impressive view of the city. The central parts of the town hall include the square complex facing the town hall square, which flanks the great hall within the building. The fact that the hall is really an open square covered with glass becomes clear when you look at this air photo.

At the bottom of the picture you can see the remains of the old town hall garden, which was heavily reduced when H. C. Andersens Boulevard was established in the 1950s. On the other side of the town hall tower, the street of Løngangsstræde leads to the city jail and the court building (the old town hall) that are connected by the "bridge of sighs".

The great hall of the town hall – the city's grandest meeting place – is actually a covered square. The building to the right houses the city archives and city council's meeting rooms. The building to the left houses the rooms for entertaining guests, with access to the balcony facing the town hall square.

Colour in focus

The Palads cinema centre and the railway pit at Vesterport station from three different angles. Here, Copenhagen's second railway station was placed (1864-1911).

When the station was closed, the two open ends of the hall were walled up and a cinema established in the huge room. The present cinema opened in the era of silent pictures (1918). Palads has seen both ups and downs, but has survived them, being the only classic Copenhagen cinema to do so. This is probably due to a major renovation (1978) that turned the cinema into a multi-cinema with 12 cinemas in one, which made the cinema the world's largest of its kind. The decoration of the building's facades lends a colourful touch to the city's image, supplemented by the omnipresent yellow busses. The decoration was designed by Poul Gernes (1989).

55°40'34.22"N   12°33'48.43"E

Søpavillonen
– the pavilion on the lake

It looks like an oversized Swedish cottage with an oriental touch in the form of the two minaret-like towers.

Vilhelm Dahlerup's pavilion at the end of the lake Peblingesøen was built in 1894 as the headquarters of the Copenhagen skating association.

That was the time of real winters. Already in 1885 the association had been permitted by the City of Copenhagen to use the southern part of the lake for its activities, and the new clubhouse contained office, board room, store room, changing room, a café and not least a separate ladies' lounge.

Opinions on the building have always varied; some find it elegant, others decidedly ugly. With its central position, it has been subject to several attacks during the years. This occurred most recently in 1979 when plans were presented for building a public swimming pool there as part of the redevelopment of the inner part of the Nørrebro quarter.

The building was completely renovated by its present owner in the middle of the 1980s and now serves as a music venue and discotheque during weekends.

The algae in the lake tell us that the temperature of the water nowadays in the summer is considerably higher than in winter at the time of the skaters.

55°40'55.05"N 12°33'33.42"E

Here was the old Nørreport gate. To the left in the inner town, Copenhageners lived crammed together from cellar to attic; to the right, people who had passed the ramparts came into sheer farm country.

Passing the old, narrow town gate was like passing a country border until 1856. In connection with the restructuring of the Copenhagen railway at the end of the 19th century, it was decided to establish a ring line around the inner city.

The Boulevard line was dug where the demolished ramparts had been, which was very practical because there were no houses there! The Boulevard line was inaugurated in 1917, connecting the Central Station with Østerport Station. On the same occasion, Nørreport station was inaugurated as Denmark's only underground station.

Nørreport station competes with the Central station for being the country's most used station. Here, several bus lines, local and regional train lines and the new metro cross each other. People are pumped up from underground, they change means of transportation or continue on foot in all directions on their way to work or to the inner city's many temptations – morning, noon and evening. Some hours later, the return trip goes in the opposite direction, again via Nørreport station – often with a much lighter wallet.

The Metro

Steel, rock and surveillance cameras. Modernity's mark on public transport. Escalators bring Copenhageners into a huge shaft. Soon a white train arrives behind armoured glass that opens mechanically on a given impulse.

The train has no driver. The time table is controlled by a computer, and the operation is monitored by men behind screens at a remote command centre.

The driverless trains run between Vanløse and Amager. Mostly underground, but on Fredriksberg and in Ørestad the trains come up into the fresh air. The new Ørestad quarter and the Metro are one and the same. Ørestad is dependent on the Metro, or perhaps it is the reverse! In any case, it is all about finances.

Plants behind glass

Our position is above the old ramparts, more specifically above the Botanical Garden close to Nørreport station. The history of the place is put into perspective in the small key map where it is clear that the lake is part of an old moat, which now is winding past rare trees and exotic plants.

The history of the Botanical Garden dates back to the time of Christian IV where it was located in the garden behind Charlottenborg (see pages 52-53) before the removal to the discarded ramparts in 1874.

Brewery owner J. C. Jacobsen and head gardener Tyge Rothe were prime movers in the building of the palm house, which was erected 1872-74 based on an English model (Crystal Palace).

The palm house is about 100 metres long and is covered by 14,000 square metres of glass. The circular greenhouse at the centre has a diameter of 30 metres and is 16 metres high. Complex mechanisms ensure different temperatures and humidity levels in the various sections of the house. Thus, we can enjoy all sorts of vegetation from various climate zones and continents like coffee trees, tea bushes, banana plants and black pepper, a wealth of different orchids and of course the palms that can be viewed from a circular "path" seven metres above the ground.

Statens Museum for Kunst
– the national art museum

The imposing museum building was designed by the architects Vilhelm Dahlerup and Georg Møller. It was built on the cleared Quitzow's bastion on the old ramparts and was inaugurated in 1896.

The wide staircase takes the museum visitor to the monumental main entrance. If the visitor turns around, he will have a magnificent view of Rosenborg castle and the park Kongens Have.

The national art museum contained the old art collection that had become homeless at the fire at Christiansborg Palace in 1884 and which was based on the kings' old private art collection that dates back

to the 16th century. The museum contains more than 8,000 paintings and works of art, including a large number of the major works from Danish artists. A modern extension was added in 1994-96; its ends can be seen on both sides at the back of the original building. Pages 132-133 show the new building from another angle.

The Østre Anlæg park contains another, smaller art museum. Opposite the national art museum you can see Den Hirschsprungske

Samling with its entrance from the street of Stockholmsgade (at the top towards the left corner). The small intimate museum opened in 1911; it bases its exhibition activities on tobacco manufacturer Heinrich Hirschsprung's private collection, which he donated to the new museum.

At the bottom right corner you can see DSB's (Danish railways) headquarters in the former Sølvgade barracks.

a big city. The old moat runs like a boomerang round Pückler's Bastion, leaving us in no doubt that this is an old fortification.

Statens Museum for Kunst makes a monumental sight in the south-eastern corner of the park with the new addition (1996-98) on the bank side at the lake. The park also serves as

visible locations in the city to end up here.

The street of Stockholmsgade forms the border of the park to the northwest, cutting diagonally from the Sølvtorvet square (lower left corner) to the Oslo Plads square. The many trees to the left in the picture grow at Holmen's churchyard.

Outside the lake area

Nordre Frihavnsgade (cutting its way from middle of the bottom to
the harbour) developed into Østerbro's working-class quarter (left). In
Frihavnen you can see the ferry to Oslo (to the extreme right) and to
the north, the Svanemølleværket power station. The big grass area in
front of the power station is the home ground of the football club
B93; previously it contained the gasworks Østre Gasværk.

Current harbour activities take place in Nordhavnen – the northern
harbour – that grows into Øresund as a result of fillings.

unloading and storing goods could take place without any cumbersome customs declaration.

Frihavnen came to be a thing of the past, and in the 1990s the harbour environment became characterised by modern houses and office complexes. At the bottom to the left we find the "Cathedral" and its two towers, an old silo, which today houses the administration of Danish Regions. On the middle peer is "Company House" whose characteristic curved form reminds you of a half cut cylinder. It was built to be the headquarters of the East Asiatic Company and now houses the insurance company Alm. Brand. On the east peer (at the top of the picture) we find Dahlerup's warehouse from 1894 (in the middle), which is the only one of its kind to have been preserved, now housing the Danish Enterprise and Construction Authority. A cruise liner and a naval ship are calling at the Langelinie quay (which was never part of Frihavnen) (at the top of the picture).

The new mermaid

The group of sculptures at the square of Ny Dahlerup Torv in Frihavnen is called the gene-modified paradise and is the result of the sculptor's sculptural complex, created for EXPO 2000 in Hanover. In 2006, the complex was placed in an area north of Dahlerup's warehouse on the Langelinie Allé avenue. The main sculpture consists of a sinking triumphal arch with a Madonna at the top, and together with a number of other sculptures it is placed in a basin with 10 centimetres of water in it. The new little mermaid, however, is placed in the east basin. It has been called a gene-modified little sister to the older one of the kind, who is situated a few hundred metres to the south. Those advocating the placing of the sculptural groups in Frihavnen find it necessary to have new cultural attractions to get people to Copenhagen, and they are also an important part in the knowledge economy that Denmark is about to become. Whatever that is

supposed to mean! Another new activity in Frihavnen is the departure of the ferry to Oslo, which departs every day at 17.00. Having been banished from Kvæsthus-broen, the huge DFDS ferries now use Frihavnen instead.

Visits

They enliven the harbour and are reminders of its heyday. Every year, about 300 large cruise liners visit Copenhagen's harbour.

Most of them moor by the Langelinie quay for a day or so before they continue with all the (mainly) American tourists.

The Langelinie quay is over 1 kilometre long and a real parade quay, which is also used by visiting naval ships, and it is here that the Copenhageners can look at spectacular newbuildings. The Langelinie quay has two levels, a promenade building with a road on the roof! (Langelinie Allé with the parked cars at the top of the picture).

Many of the promenade building's old store rooms have been turned into souvenir shops; lying like pearls on a string, they are the first thing that the one-day tourists meet in Copenhagen. Many of them do not get any further except for the required visit with the Little Mermaid sitting on her rock close by.

On the next page you can see some of the many new cars in Nordhavnen.

The Svanemølleværket power station

Svanemølleværket is situated at Kalk-brænderihavnen, being powerful and monumental in its industrial expression. Since 1953 the power station has been supplying Copenhageners with electricity and heating.

Until 1985, a flow of ships delivered huge quantities of coal to the hungry ovens at the power station. Forty boilermen worked in three shifts in the 45 metres high boiler room (the building to the left). The tall chimneys sent the carbon monoxide 100 metres into the air before it spread about the quarter. In the less tall turbine hall, generators transformed the steam into electricity. In 1985, the power station was converted to natural gas. The power station supplies electricity to 115,000 consumers and heating to 40,000 houses.

The pleasure boats are about to take over the old Kalkbrænderihavn. However, some bulk cargo is still being unloaded (stones, road stones, gravel), which the ramp at the upper left corner reminds us of. To the right in the picture we find Paustian's modern furniture house. It was designed by the architect Jørgen Utzon and his two sons, Jan and Kim, and it was erected in 1987.

Østre Gasværk
– gasworks and theatre

The huge dome-shaped building is the only remains of the Østre Gasværk gasworks that shut off the taps in 1969. The gas tank is a monument of the industrialisation of Copenhagen.

Martin Nyrup (Copenhagen's town hall) designed the big gas tank whose impressive dome rests on a thick circular wall with an outside diameter of 47 metres.

Østre Gasværk was provided with coal from the harbour via the gasworks' own small railway whose construction might very well remind you of a rollercoaster.

In 1979, the gas tank opened as a theatre. The impressive remnant from Copenhagen's industrialisation is one of Denmark's most spectacular and evocative auditoriums. It has lent stage to a number of musicals like "Les Miserables" and "Miss Saigon". The rest of the gasworks site is now either fields (the upper right corner of the picture) or the football pitches of the football club B 93 (see pages 136-137).

Fælledparken
– the common park

The city's green lung is part of the large cor
previously covered the area north of the tov
Here, the sheep grazed, and the army was
1911, Fælledparken was inaugurated as a pu
main entrance was never made; it was agains
the park should be accessible from all angles.
number of buildings on the fringe of the park
the Blegdamsvej road (in the lower right corn
inner part of the Øster Allé avenue (perpendic
Parken sports centre) – prevent this, and in th
only enter the park via the entrance at the Tri
(in the middle to the extreme right).

The many buildings of Rigshospitalet, the n
cover quite a bit of the old common area at t
the picture, just like the Parken sports centre
side of Øster Allé. Fælledparken is synonymou
which became popular in the years when the
established. Several legendary Copenhagen c
as a result of the play with the ball on the cor
instance B 1903 and AB, which had their pitc
opposite side of the Nørre Allé avenue that le
lower left corner towards the Vibenhus Rund
In 1960, this part of the common was used fo
related to the University of Copenhagen's scie

Idrætsparken, Copenhagen's largest footba
inaugurated as the Danish national arena in 1

The latest major reconstruction took place a
of the 1990s. Parken provides an evocative se
42,000 spectators gather around the grass fo
national soccer team's matches. It can accom
more when it comes to concerts with famous

But first and foremost, Fælledparken is the
Here, you can do (nearly) anything, and this
Copenhageners have done for almost 100 ye
park is still the natural meeting place for mor
"demonstrators" (depending on the weather
May, the international labour day.

Circus in town

The city does not leave much room for touring circuses. An area at the Bellahøj quarter is a permanent circus site, and the of course there is the public Fælledpark.

Cirkus Dannebrog has put up its tents, and the army of circus wagons and caravans lends colour to the corner of the streets of Blegdamsvej and Øster Alle. The next couple of evenings, music will fill the big tent to accompany the artists' neck-breaking performance, the clowning and the animal trainers' cracks of their whips; then the circus will pack and continue its tour of the country to entertain children and other enthusiasts. In the lower left corner you can see part of the Østerbro post office.

Rigshospitalet
- the national hospital

Rigshospitalet takes up quite a bit of space, and the high central complex can be seen from far away.

In 2007, Rigshospitalet celebrated its 150th anniversary as its history dates back to the establishment of "Det Kongelige Frederiks Hospital" in the street of Bredgade in 1757. From 1905 to 1910 the new national hospital was built at Blegdams common. The hospital consisted of a large number of pavilions around a court. Space quickly became scarce, but it was not until 1960 that the reconstruction and extension really started. It was to last 18 years! In 1970, the large central complex opened, and the work was completed in 1978. The original, beautiful main entrance faced the street of Blegdamsvej, where there is a lawn today (in the middle of the picture to the extreme right).

Rigshospitalet was also the university hospital. Today, the medical faculty resides at the Panum Institute with the funny, coloured, chimney-like pipes on the roof (bottom). The roof of Rigshospitalet is being converted into a helicopter platform.

Østerbro

In the 16th century, "the black dam" was established along the street of Østerbrogade at the far end of the lake. A complex system of damming and stream regulations was to supply Copenhagen with water for drinking and for filling the moat. And the dammed water was not supposed to run into Øresund; hence the dam.

Thus, the Copenhagen lakes are not natural, but dammed, and they got their basin-like shape in connection with a major clean-up in 1725-27.

Along the north-western side of the lake of Sortedams Søen (left) runs the Dosseringen embankment boasting posh, luxurious flats with a lake view and morning sun. In contrast, we find the street of Ryesgade with its many tenement houses only 100 metres away (to the left) parallel with Dosseringen; the bourgeoisie and the working class living almost as next-door neighbours.

On the south-eastern side of the lake (to the right), the quarter of Kartoffelrækkerne is quite dominant. The 480 houses on 11 dead-straight, parallel streets were established as building society houses from 1873 to 1889 in an area that had previously been used for growing potatoes (potato=kartoffel). Built as a social provision for poor working-class families. Today, an exclusive enclave in the city that especially attracts well-educated people with somewhat leftwing views, but with wallets of a certain size. We can feel the area's special intimacy on the next page where we have moved a little closer.

The green area to the right is the churchyard Holmens Kirkegård.

The hen and the egg

It was especially the area around Rådhuspladsen and Vesterports Passage that from 1925 was provided with brightly coloured neon signs.

Of course, the centre of the city with its massive concentration of attractions had to be illuminated day and night, up-to-date with the latest city fads.

However, the surrounding quarters also wished to emphasize their own identity with smaller, local neon signs. At the entrance to Nørrebro, a number of advertisements for the Irma supermarket chain throw an evocative neon light on the Peblingesøen lake, creating impressive reflections in the water..

The egg-laying Irma hen is probably Copenhagen's most well-known neon sign. It did not begin to lay eggs until 1936. In 1950, the eggs were made larger, and in 1953 the hen was replaced with a new one of its kind, which since then has laid millions of coloured eggs.

Nørrebro

The churchyard and park, Assistens Kirkegård, is like a green oasis in the middle of the densely populated quarter of Nørrebro. Our perspective means that the old working-class quarter seems more green than it does when viewed at street level. Like its name indicates, Assistens Kirkegård was established around 1760 as a relief churchyard, far outside the capital's ramparts.

It still functions as a churchyard, but is also a kind of churchyard museum where a large number of famous Danes, led by Hans Christian Andersen, are buried. The churchyard is being used as a public park for the quarter's inhabitants, and during the summer, it provides the setting for activities that take place in no other churchyard in the country.

To the north, the area is flanked by Nørrebrogade, which as the quarter's main street cuts across the picture towards the lake area and the centre to the right. The street of Jagtvej lies as if drawn with a ruler from the lower left corner, crossing Frederiksberg to the crossroads of Vibenhus Runddel and then splitting into an inner part (to the right) and an outer part (to the left).

In the bottom right corner is the area that was once misleadingly called Rabarberlandet (rhubarb country). Before the slum clearance started in the 1970s, this was one of Copenhagen's worst slum areas, in fierce competition with the similarly completely renovated Sorte Firkant (black square) (to the right of Assistens Kirkegård).

Making room for courtyards

Bispeengbuen
– a motor traffic street

It originates from the time when motor traffic streets were the latest fad in big modern cities.

The car people and quite of lot of town hall politicians looked forward to the establishment of a lake ring (a motor traffic street project along the lakes), and other Los Angeles-like projects were prepared.

The establishment of Bispeengbuen was one of the only projects to actually be carried through. A lot of people today probably consider this fortunate.

The motor traffic street winds like a reverse S, taking cars coming from the Borups Allé avenue to third-floor height and leading them into the street of Ågade and further on towards the centre of Copenhagen. Bispeengbuen has six lanes that are used daily by more than 50,000 cars. Ågade is situated on top of the stream of Ladegårdsåen, which is led through pipes below the street towards the Peblingesøen lake, marking the border between the district of Frederiksberg (to the far right) and the quarter of Nørrebro.

We have the grand view of Nørrebro seen from west to east. In the middle of the picture you can see the outer part of the quarter, and at the lakes we find the inner part of Nørrebro. The quarter's main street Nørrebrogade cuts diagonally from the left in its course to the lakes, on its way flanking the Assistens Kirkegård churchyard (the large green area in the middle of the picture). The other, somewhat smaller, green area closer to the photographer is the Nørrebro Park, which is located in a former railway area.

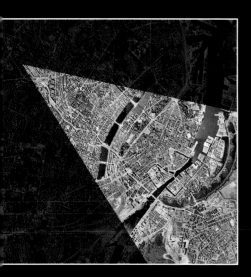

Frederiksberg's town hall

Frederiksberg is an independent municipality surrounded by Copenhagen on all sides. A town within the city. There has always been a special atmosphere on this "autonomous island" in the middle of greater Copenhagen.

From time to time, the municipality wishes to emphasize the quarter's special status, for instance in the form of distinctive street furniture, which is clearly different from what Copenhagen has.

And of course Frederiksberg had to have a suitable town hall. The location was decided upon in 1941, and the work started in earnest after the German occupation. The town hall, which is one of Denmark's largest municipal buildings, was inaugurated in 1953.

The big, five-storey redbrick building has a tower, which is 60 metres high and whose glass construction makes you think of a lighthouse. The tower faces the street of Smallegade, which ends in Frederiksberg's town hall square at the bottom of the picture. The street continues towards the centre of Copenhagen under the name of Gammel Kongevej.

The street of Frederiksberg Bredegade runs along the opposite side of the town hall. The street is a small remnant of the ancient road between Copenhagen and Roskilde, whose original curve can be seen from the position of the yellow building at the top of the picture.

The hill of Valby Bakke

We are right above Valby Bakke, the only hilly landscape in the central part of greater Copenhagen. The new king Frederik IV was perhaps exaggerating a little when he renamed the hill Frederiksberg (Frederik's mountain) in connection with the erection from 1699 of a new palace at the top of the hill. The new palace was of course surrounded by a suitable palace garden established according to the strict baroque requirements for symmetry and order in nature. One transverse axis of the garden can still be clearly seen in the form of the continuing grass areas stretching on both sides of the palace from the park of Søndermarken (in the lower part of the picture) and through the park of Frederiksberg Have towards north on the other side of the palace.

The road from Copenhagen to Roskilde was moved in 1772 to the hill close to the palace and can be seen in its horizontal course across the picture. It divided the palace garden into Søndermarken and Frederiksberg Have. Around 1800, both gardens were restructured to become English landscape gardens.

At the foot of the hill, a new part of town emerged, which was named after the palace: Frederiksberg.

Frederiksberg Palace

It was built as a pleasure palace for the despot king Frederik IV.

The original miniature palace from 1699 was extended from 1707 to 1709 to a real baroque palace in the form of the wing at the top of the picture.

In connection with subsequent extensions, the palace got its present quadratic character where the wall facing Roskildevej with the main gate curves a little.

The palace was used frequently by Frederik IV in the first two decades of the 18th century. Christian VI lived here in the 1730s during the building of Christiansborg Palace, and it was here that Struense enjoyed the company of Queen Caroline Mathilde around 1770. The palace had its final heyday under Frederik VI at the beginning of the 19th century.

It was during this period that palace gardens were changed from imposing baroque gardens into landscapes in the modern English style. In this connection, the characteristic canals were dug and the garden was provided with various temples, grottos and exotic summerhouses. Thus, at the top of the picture you can see the Chinese summerhouse built by the royal architect Andreas Kirketerp in 1799.

When property had to be divided in connection with the transition from despotism to democracy, the palace and the garden became the property of the Danish state. The garden was opened to the public, and the palace has housed the Danish military academy since 1868.

Zoologisk Have
– the Copenhagen zoo

After the royal family had relinquished Frederiksberg Palace in 1852, the ornithologist Niels Kjærbølling installed himself in 1859 in a small part of the old palace garden to the west of the palace where he displayed rare animals. Following several extensions, Zoologisk Have became one of Copenhagen's major attractions. It is being modernised on a continuous basis, allowing the well over 3500 animals to be observed in realistic surroundings.

The bears live in the rocky area in the upper right corner, whereas the apes and monkeys enjoy themselves in the monkey and ape house and in the outside grottos at the top to the left.

The zoo tower is 43 metres high. Added to the 30 metres of Valby Bakke, the adventurous mountaineer gets 75 metres up to an excellent view of large parts of central Copenhagen.

The tower was inaugurated in 1905 as a miniature version of the Eiffel tower.

Frederiksberg from another angle

A view of outer Frederiksberg from an alternative angle. At the bottom of the picture, blocks of flats around the streets of Dalgas Boulevard and Finsensvej. From the lower left corner, the metro runs diagonally towards the right. The area north of the tracks previously contained a lot of industrial businesses, but now it is dominated by modern houses and educational institutions. Thus, the long, white building contains one of the Copenhagen Business School's many branches, whereas the two horseshoe buildings behind are the housing complex Dalgas Have. The tall, white chimney marks the headquarters of Frederiksberg Forsyning (gas, water, electricity and heating) and to the left a major part of the municipality's extensive area with detached houses.

The telephone house (to the left of the middle) marks the border between Frederiksberg and Nørrebro.

Carlsberg and hops town

The Carlsberg brewery's extensive complex of buildings at Valby Bakke is like a monument for Copenhagen as an industrial city. During the establishment of Denmark's first railway, a spring had been found at Valby Bakke. Brewery owner J. C. Jacobsen therefore decided to move his brewery from the street of Brolæggerstræde within the still existing ramparts to the open country and the pure water at Valby Bakke. He named the new brewery after his son Carl.

In 1847, the first successful brewing was carried out at what was later to be known as Gammel Carlsberg, old Carlsberg (to the extreme left). For almost 150 years, Carlsberg was one of Denmark's largest industrial workplaces, and the last big one to close down in central Copenhagen.

These years, the area is being transformed into an exciting new residential area in contrast to the old workmen's houses. The building society houses are called Humlebyen (hops town) because of the smell that previously characterised the area.

Vesterbro

Again, we are above Valby Bakke, only this time the photographer has turned his camera 45 degrees east as compared with the picture on pages 172-173, and we get an overall view of the old working-class quarter of Vesterbro in the area south of the lakes (the right fourth of the picture).

The clear weather helps us get the overall view. In the distance, Øresund (the Sound) and the harbour to which Copenhagen owes its existence. Along the lower part of the right edge you can see the innermost parts of the large railway area that follows the original beach. A little to the left, Søndre Boulevard curves towards the centre of Copenhagen. The boulevard was established in the area that from 1847 saw the first trains from Copenhagen to Roskilde; the air photo gives you a good indication of this.

At the bottom of the picture is Carlsberg's large plant at the foot of Valby Bakke and above are the Enghave Park and the Enghave Plads square, from whose one end, the street of Istedgade shoots like a straight line through the heart of Vesterbro towards Hovedbanegården, the central station.

To the left in the picture, from the bottom you can see the central part of Frederiksberg, then Nørrebro and at the top, Østerbro, where the power station Svanemølleværket's 100 metres high chimneys form the border towards Øresund.

The harbour

A unique view of Copenhagen's harbour seen towards north-east. The harbour winds from the south harbour (at the bottom of the picture) through the inner harbour towards the north harbour.

The sea fort Tre Kroner (right above the clouds of steam) marks the traditional border between the harbour and Øresund.

The boilers at the H. C. Ørstedsværket power station are running at full capacity. In the foreground, the new combined bridge for pedestrians and bicycles connects the Fisketorvet shopping centre with Islands Brygge (see pages 188-189). Islands Brygge (to the right of the harbour) has undergone dramatic changes in recent years, and today it is like a completely new quarter of the city. The Langebro bridge marks the border between the south harbour and the inner harbour, whereas the Knippelsbro bridge is only partly visible in the middle of the picture. Even at very long distance, the opera house and Burmeister & Wain's old assembly building at Refshaleøen take up a fair amount of space in the picture.

At the end of the new bridge Bryggebroen (see pages 188-189), you can see the seeds silo (see pages 190-191), an example of an old industrial plant that has been converted into spectacular luxury flats. We are in "Havnestaden", which has arisen on Islands Brygge, partly on the former soy bean cake factory's site at the harbour.

Large iron structures have been mounted on the outside of the old seeds silo as bands that optimise light and the view in the 84 luxury flats that have been made in the 39 metres silo at the foot of the new bridge over the harbour. Today, the seeds silo is called Gemini Residence.

The H. C. Ørstedsværket power station

The city craved energy. The power station H. C. Ørstedsværket started to be used in 1920 as Denmark's first really big electricity plant. It was built on filled-up areas made for this purpose in Copenhagen's south harbour, which was about to become a bulk harbour.

Just like the power stations of Østre Gasværk and later Svanemølleværket, it was placed close to the harbour to allow the coal ships to call at the door and to secure access to cooling water.

H. C. Ørstedsværket produced alternating current and was thus a precondition for the city's large industrial businesses' ability to replace steam engines with electric engines as the source of power in the manufacturing process.

The power station underwent a lot of renovations and additions, and in 1932 it was provided with a spare diesel engine built at Burmeister & Wain (height 13 metres, length 13 metres). For 35 years it was the largest diesel engine in the world and today it is still the main attraction at the industrial museum DieselHouse that resides in the red building in the lower left corner.

The power station was involved in one of the most serious air crashes in Denmark. On the 15 of August, 1957, 23 people died when a Russian plane collided with one of the station's chimneys and crashed into the harbour.

Bryggebroen bridge

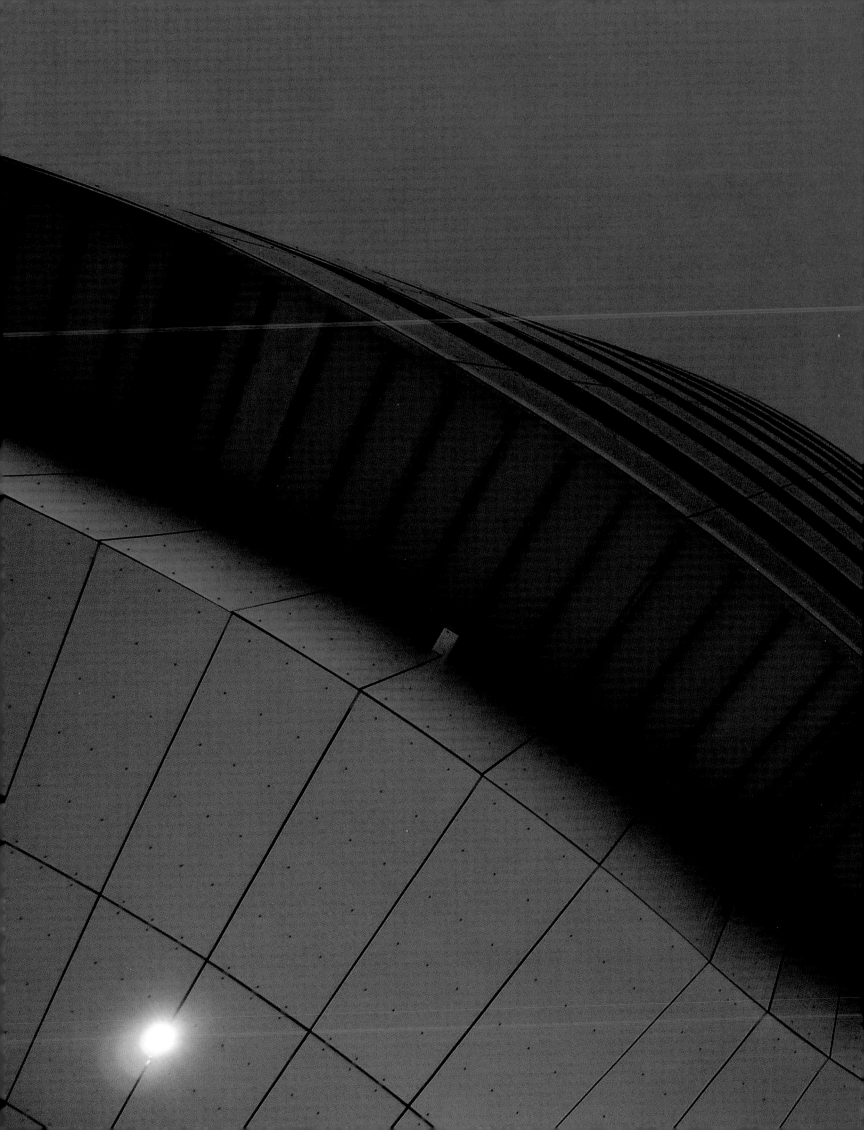

The seeds silo – Gemini Residence

The harbour swimming bath

The picture can fully document the revitalisation that Islands Brygge has been through during the past decade. Even though we are only a few hundred metres from the town hall square, Islands Brygge has been living its own somewhat slighted and isolated life most of the time. This quarter of Copenhagen is situated on a filled-up area which was not developed until 1905 and which was quickly characterised by noisy and polluting companies with the soy bean cake factory Dansk Soyakagefabrik as the predominant one of its kind. The wide quay area was covered with railway wagons, cranes and heaps of coal, and the dust clouds shrouded Islands Brygge, accompanied by the noise from goods wagons being pulled and supplemented by the smell of soy bean cakes.

After the harbour activities had been discontinued, Islands Brygge's activists took over the quay and transformed it into a kind of public park at the inhabitants' own premise in glaring contrast to the dreary office buildings on the opposite side of the harbour (outside the picture).

On a sunny summer Sunday, the area is fully papered with people and the harbour swimming bath has a magnetic effect. When you think of the water quality in Copenhagen's harbour just 20 years ago, it is difficult to understand that it is sufficiently pure today for swimming in it. In both senses a success story. The harbour swimming bath opened in 2002.

The island of Amager

An overall view of the northern part of Amager seen from the south.

At the bottom to the left, the road of Amager Fælledvej winds towards the centre of Copenhagen, following Amager's ancient coast line to the west.

The area to the left of the road is therefore situated on the former seabed. DR Byen, the Danish broadcasting corporation takes up quite a bit of space in the curve at the bottom to the left. You can see Amagerbrogade as a long line going diagonally through the picture, making it to its edge, a little above the lower right corner, and continuing as Amager Landevej towards the town of Dragør. At all times, these roads have been the main axis and artery on Amager. The Englandsvej road can be seen in the middle of the picture. Opposite Sundby football ground (at the bottom of the picture) are the white blocks of flats called Urbanplanen, whose establishment was initiated by Copenhagen's mayor at the time, Urban Hansen.

The large areas with detached houses are being replaced by fairly old blocks of flats the closer we get to the centre. To the north, the Kløvermarken area can be seen as a green spot. Today a football stronghold, once the end station for the city's refuse and later the place where the first aircraft enthusiasts flew in their primitive aircraft.

At the top of the island is the Amagerværket power station. This power station was built at the beginning of the 1970s and is now owned by Swedish Vattenfall. It supplies 100,000 homes with heating and covers 20% of Zealand's electricity consumption (see pages 198-199).

Wind power

Here at Middelgrunden, the water depth is only 2 to 6 metres. In 2000/01 20 windmills were erected in this shallow area. They stand in a curved row, 180 metres apart. The wind power is gathered in the mill in the middle from which a submarine cable takes the power to the Amagerværket power station (see the next pages). In the background the fort at Middelgrunden was established in 1890-94 on soil that was dug and carried out here in connection with the establishment of Frihavnen, the free port.

It is the world's largest island created by man without a permanent connection to shore. The mills stand in about the same place where Lord Nelson's English fleet on 2nd April, 1801, lay in a long row, gunning the Dano-Norwegian fleet that lay in similar line closer to shore (to the extreme left in the picture) during the battle of Copenhagen.

The mills that have undeniably added a new silhouette to the entrance to Copenhagen's harbour, cover about 3% of the Copenhageners' electricity requirements.

The SAS hotel

This is the oldest of a large number of monumental buildings that have come to flank Amager Boulevard on its course towards the Langebro bridge. SAS Hotel Scandinavia was built in 1973 as Denmark's largest international hotel with 542 rooms.

The location is perfect, close to the city centre and not far from the airport in Kastrup. With its 86 metres, the hotel is one of the capital's highest buildings, and the top floors therefore have a magnificent view of Christianshavn and the harbour on one side and Ørestad and the Amager Fælled common on the other.

In the top left corner of the picture you can see the top of Panterens Bastion on Christianshavns Vold.

The Tietgen residence hall

"We have got the most beautiful residence hall in the world," said the chairman of the residence hall's board at the inauguration of the building. And it is true that we must characterise the residence hall as the most spectacular new building in Ørestad with its wealth of exciting details. Very few round buildings are being built so the architects from the firm of Lundgaard & Tranberg had to go all the way to China to find inspiration in the Tulou buildings, a village cooperative gathered in circular buildings.

The circular residence hall with seven floors consists of five sections separated by vertical walls that functionally and visually divide the hall. At street level there is access from the five sections to the central courtyard.

The residence hall opened in 2006 and consists of 360 student rooms that are situated on the outer side, whereas the areas facing the courtyard are used for various kinds of common rooms, supplemented by open terraces facing the courtyard.

The Tietgen residence hall is located in the inner part of Ørestad at Emil Holms Kanal, right next to the University of Copenhagen.

DR Byen

These new headquarters for the Danish broadcasting corporation DR have for many years been the most mentioned building work in the country, and the most extensive building scandal.

The complex consists of four segments. Along the Metro track is segment 3 which is the domicile of Copenhagen's radio, to the right is segment 4 – the big blue building - the concert hall. The massive exceeding of the building budgets is mainly due to the construction of this concert hall, which is designed by the French architect Jean Nouvel. It can accommodate 1800 people and is constructed so as to give the impression that it hovers at a height of 15 metres. Behind the concert hal is segment 1 with the large studios, segment 2 with the news studio, where news programmes for both TV and radio have their basis. A long glass passage runs through the complex like a main road, connecting segments 1 and 2 with segments 3 and 4 on its course over Emil Holms Kanal. At the left of segment 2 are the IT University and the Tietgen residence hall (see page 201).

The metro is winding like an S to the left towards Ørestaden. The car park at the right of the picture is probably one of Denmark's most windswept areas.

In its monumental expression, DR Byen is an anachronism. Its signal is that DR should have a leading position in society and be a dominant factor in the overall media picture. But this is a position from which the institution has long since been ousted and which it will never regain, despite the new headquarters.

55°39'29.89"N 12°35'27.27"E

55°37'53.02"N 12°34'48.58"E

Ørestad

Copenhagen's new quarter Ørestad is really beginning to assume its character. Ideas were big at the beginning of the 1990s, and for once, the visions have been realized.

The basic idea was to create a completely new, modern quarter with space and room for new buildings on a large scale, in accordance with an overall plan. A mixture of educational institutions, businesses, office buildings and residential areas combined with cultural attractions in a green environment was to position not only Copenhagen, but the entire Øresund region as a centre of growth in the ever increasing competition about the future's workplaces.

Ørestad is built on the innermost part of the old common as an elongated rectangle (310 hectares). In the background is Amager's coastline. Ørestad is built on the former seabed, which makes special demands on the construction of the buildings' foundations.

We are above the southern part of Ørestad, which we are observing with our backs turned west. The metro and Ørestads Boulevard cut like a common axis through Ørestad in their close, parallel courses. The transport corridor across Amager crosses this axis perpendicularly at Ørestad Station close to Ferring's 20-storey tower block. Opposite, across the boulevard, is the enormous shopping centre Fields. In the left corner of the picture you can see an example of the experimenting building of flats, which is also characteristic of Ørestad. Down in the right corner you can see the construction of the engineering company Rambøll's new headquarters and the new hotel "Crown Plaza Towers".

The street of Amagerbrogade

Amagerbrogade is 3.4 kilometres long and it has undergone few changes in recent years.

In the middle of the picture you can see the churchyard Frelsers Kirkegård. The blocks of flats on the right side of Amagerbrogade south of the churchyard (at the bottom of the picture) are considerably older than those at the top of the picture (towards the city centre). This oddity is due to the fact that until 1909 Christianshavns Vold was a fortification area where guns had to have a free field of fire up to the churchyard! A provision that was abolished on the Zealand side in the 19th century. Thus, it was not possible to build north of the churchyard until after 1909, despite its position closer to the city centre.

Amagerbrogade extends into the street of Torvegade at Christianshavns Vold to the north (outside the top of the picture). Amager Boulevard (1907) branches out to the left in its course towards the Langebro bridge.

In the upper right corner we find the building "Møllelængen", built on the old Amagerbro Station's area in 1939 as the (then) longest block of flats in Northern Europe.

55°39'49.94"N 12°36'3.39"E

On our way to the airport

We are looking due east. The motorway and the railway cut across Amager in their courses towards the airport and the Øresund bridge, dividing not only the town of Tårnby, but the entire island into two parts.

Following quite a lot of political turbulence, money was allocated for roofing the transport corridor in the central part of Tårnby opposite Vinkelhusene (to the left in the picture). Of course, the roofing means a great deal for Tårnby's cohesion, and the citizens can look forward to a super-fast train connection to Hovedbanegården, the central station, from the station situated below the roofing.

The Englandsvej road runs from left to right at the bottom of the picture, and an IC3 train is on its way to the airport and has just passed the bridge that takes the Amager Landevej across the transport corridor further to the east (towards the top of the picture).

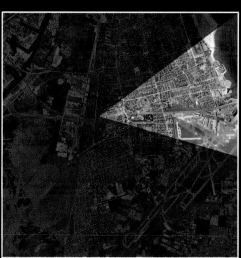

Airport

The gate to all the world is only 8 kilometres from the town hall square at the east coast of Amager. The first aircraft enthusiasts had performed their neck-breaking exercises from their base at Kløvermarken (see pages 194-195). In 1925, the young men and their planes moved to a field in Kastrup, which was soon to be used by the emerging scheduled traffic (from 1939 Copenhagen's airport). Since then the activities in the airport have developed in one direction only, upwards, also literally. In recent years the expansion has almost exploded. Copenhagen's airport is the largest in the Nordic region with 800 departures and arrivals every day. 20 million people leave or land on what is also Denmark's largest workplace with 20,000 staff.

The amount of asphalt and concrete and the number of hangars, terminals, gates and other installations have increased in direct proportion to the popularity of aviation. The airport is therefore a widespread and elongated complex of buildings, which is completely impossible to get a grasp of.

Terminal 1 stretches diagonally from the lower right corner some hundred metres parallel with the motorway. It was established in 1969 as the centre of the domestic traffic. In the middle of the picture is terminal 2, which was for many years the only international terminal. In 1998 it was relieved by terminal 3, whose curved roof, columns and large glass sections can be seen in the middle of the small picture.

In Øresund lies Peberholmen, which is an artificial island built in connection with the establishment of a permanent connection across Øresund. In the upper corners you can see the island of Saltholm (to the left) and the town of Dragør (to the right).

The connection to Sweden

Symbolically, it was inaugurated at the beginning of the new millennium. On the 1st of July 2000, the Danish and the Swedish royal families inaugurated the permanent connection across Øresund.

In the picture showing the airport (see pages 210-211) you can see that the connection is led through a 4.1 kilometre tunnel from the coast of Amager to the artificial island of Peberholmen. Here, the railway and the motorway come up into the fresh air (picture to the left seen east-west) and continue for 4.1 kilometres "on shore" until the trains go below the motorway bridge like into a crawl way. 22 spans take us to the main bridge, which is constructed as a cable-stayed bridge whose pylons reach 204 metres into the air. Having passed another 27 spans, we reach the coast of Scania south of Malmø.

55°35'53.67"N 12°45'15.00"E

The total length of the connection is 16 kilometres, of which the bridge construction takes up 7.8 kilometres. After a slow start, the traffic across the bridge is now increasing, and in 2007, 30 million cars have crossed the bridge. The connection is invaluable to the integration in the Øresund region and to the relations between the two old sister cities Copenhagen and Malmø. As a symbol of the integration, the official name of the connection is: Øresundsbron! A mixture of Danish and Swedish.

Allotments, Brøndby

The outskirts

The Avedøreværket power station

Fifty years ago, all that was here was a few flat islands in the middle of the Kalvebod channel. Avedøre Holme was established when industrial companies in the city could no longer have their space requirements fulfilled. Thus, the industrial area emerged as a result of a huge damming project in the 1960s, and today it constitutes the country's largest cohesive industrial area with about 9000 jobs. The Avedøreværket power station is the area's landmark.

It consists of two blocks, Avedøre 1 from 1990 and Avedøre 2 from 2001. The power station produces electricity and district heating, and employs 80 staff. Block 1 is coal-fired, whereas block 2 utilises the energy from oil, bio fuel and natural gas. The tall, white silos are used for storing excess hot water in periods with a low consumption of heating.

The power station is situated at the coast. Above it, parts of the large industrial area at Avedøre Holme and at the top you can see the original coastline flanking Hvidovre.

At the top to the right, you can see the gas tower in Valby.

The Arken museum of art

The Arken museum of art is located on a tongue at Ishøj Strand in the beach park of Køge Bugt.

The museum for modern art was inaugurated in 1996 with the purpose of providing the culturally under-supplied western region of Copenhagen with a counterpart to Northern Zealand's Louisiana. The spectacular exhibition building is designed by Søren Robert Lund. It would seem as if there is a good chance of combining the art experience with a fresh ducking in the waves of Køge Bugt.

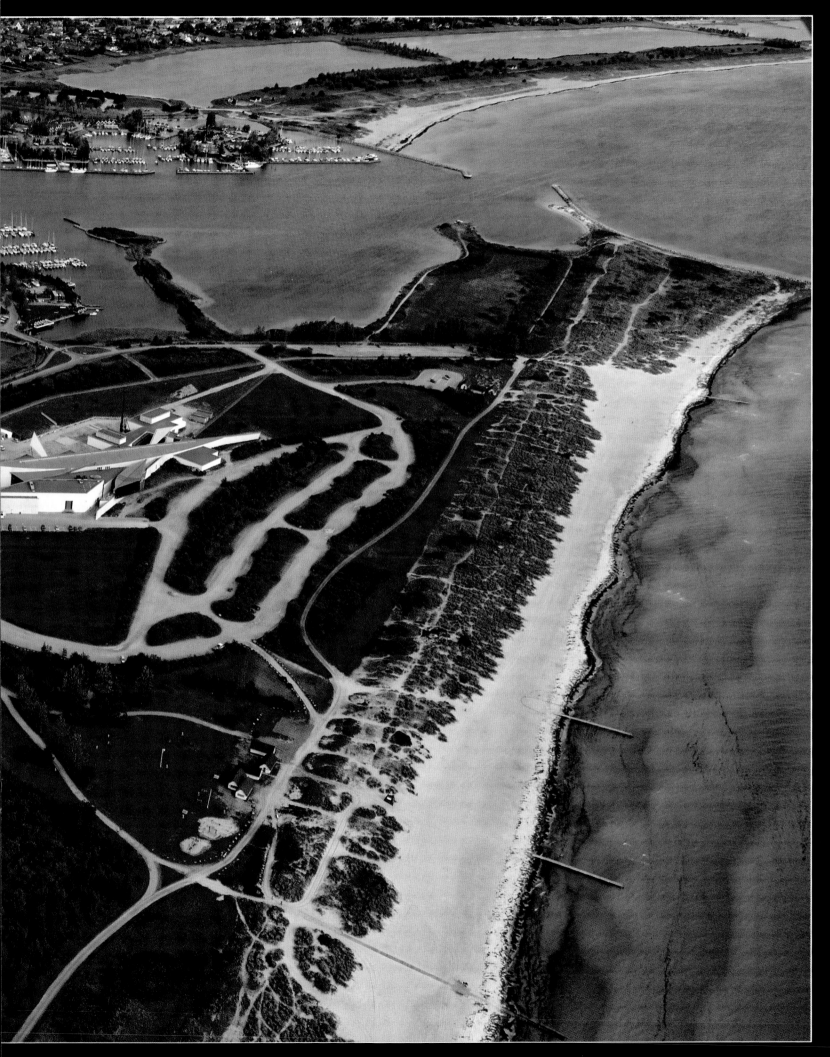

The Damhussøen lake

3.6 kilometres lies ahead of the brisk pedestrian if he wishes to walk around the lake of Damhussøen. If the trip is extended by a tour of Damhusengen, the green area north of the lake, another 2.6 kilometres awaits him. Together, the lake and the green area offer a large recreational breathing space in a part of the city that is not overflowing with green areas.

Damhussøen is an artificial lake. It was established through a damming along the road of Roskildevej (the lower embankment of the lake in the picture) of the stream of Harrestrup Å. It runs from the north through Damhusengen and its water is forced towards east into the stream of Grøndalsåen (the green braiding in the middle at the right side of the picture) and further on towards the Copenhagen lakes.

This construction dates back to the beginning of the 16th century. The purpose was to provide Copenhagen's moats with water, and for centuries the lake was also a water reservoir. North-east of the lake (in the upper right part of the picture) we find Vanløse, which is divided by the dead straight road of Ålekistevej. The eastern part of this quarter is characterised by blocks of flats, whereas detached houses are predominant in the western part towards the lake. Vanløse assumed its character in the interwar period.

To the west of the lake (in the left part of the picture) we find Rødovre, which is an independent municipality that was developed only after the second world war. To the north (at the top of the picture) you can see the Herlev hospital – Denmark's tallest building.

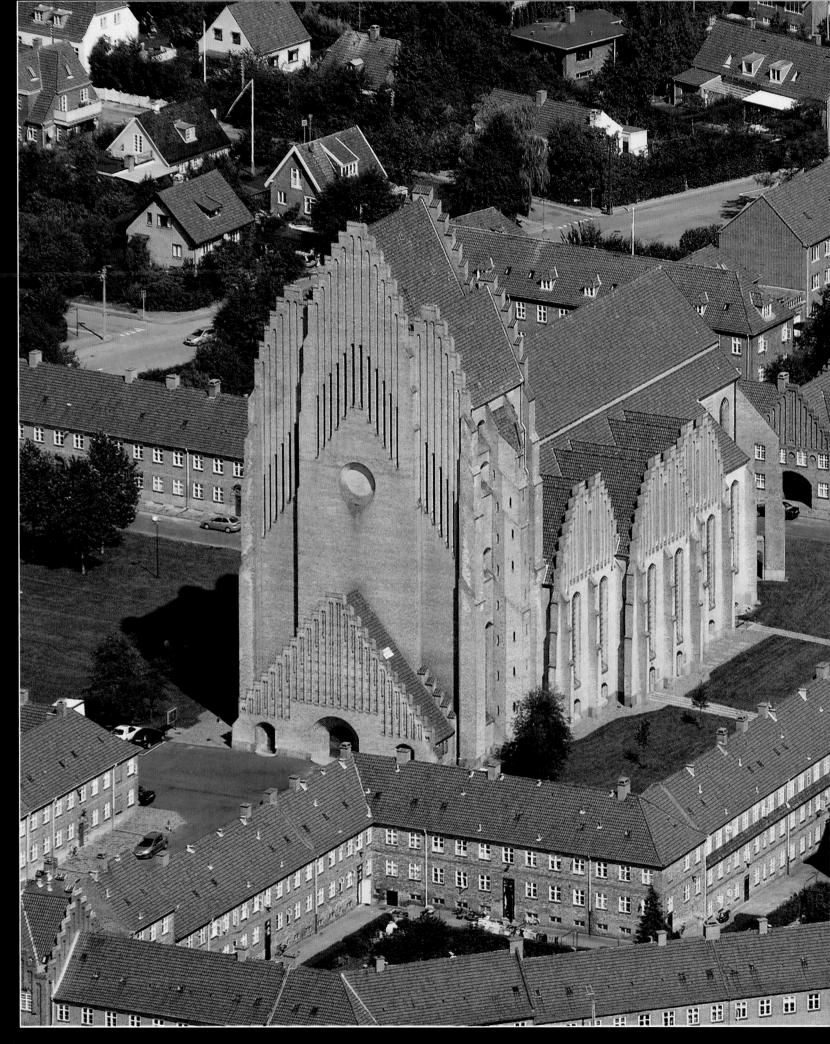

The Grundtvigskirken church

Actually, it is a bit strange that this magnificent cathedral came to form the centre of the paragon of social-democratic buildings that emerged at Bispebjerg in the interwar period. The church and Christianity were not exactly the labour movement's strongest cup of tea. There are hardly many left today who wonder about this because the church is the natural centre of the extensive yellow-brick buildings on one of the city's highest hills. The church was designed by P. V. Jensen-Klint in 1921 and he also started to build it. After his death in 1930, his son Kaare Klint took over the work, which was completed in 1940.

The magnificent basilica, which with its 2000 seats is Denmark's largest church, was erected in memory of N. F. S. Grundtvig and was funded via a national collection. About 6 million yellow hand-moulded bricks went into the building both outside and inside, which was to maintain the impression of an over-sized Danish Gothic village church.

Grundtvigskirken is a national monument and an impressive piece of architecture, whose tower construction with organ pipes reaching for the sky can be seen from large parts of the city.

Bellahøj

The author of these lines can vaguely remember when they were built. And I do remember the mentioning of the new "skyscrapers" at Bellahøj. Today, they no longer look quite so huge.

The Bellehøj blocks are situated on the highest hill in the City of Copenhagen, close to the place where the Swedish king camped before storming Copenhagen in 1659. These were the first high-rise buildings that were erected in Denmark. We are in the first half of the 1950s. The 28 individual buildings were made as prefabricated constructions in functional style. The rent of DKK 30 per square metre was just as high as the buildings. In return, the residents had a fantastic view of Copenhagen and modern flats with all the latest modernity: dining kitchens, refrigerators and electric stoves.

Brønshøj church

Brønshøj church is the oldest building in the City of Copenhagen. It was erected in Roman style from light chalk ashlar blocks by Bishop Absalon in the 1180s. The 25 metres Gothic tower was erected in red bricks around 1450, and the porch was not added until 1892.

Until 100 years ago, the church was located in the country as the centre of the village of Brønshøj, which was incorporated in the City of Copenhagen in 1901. During the Swedish siege of Copenhagen in 1658-59, the church was used as an ammunition and weapons store for the enemy's large military camp "Karlstad" at Bellahøj.

The English also camped in the churchyard during their siege of the capital in 1807.

Today, the church is situated close to the Brønshøj Torv square as a gateway to the large rather old residential area that stretches towards the green area of Utterslev Mose to the left in the picture.

Brønshøj church

Herlev hospital

With its 120 metres, Herlev hospital is Denmark's tallest building (so far).

The tall bed section of 25 storeys can be seen from most of the city. The building commenced in 1966 and was seen at the time to be a symbol of the welfare state's capability and the expanding public sector's unlimited growth potential.

During the building of the hospital, there were scandals and exceeded budgets, and at the inauguration in 1976, only the 16 storeys at the bottom could be used. The fan-shaped building at the bottom of the bed section contains lecture rooms, whereas the large four-storey building to the left in the picture is used for examinations and treatment.

The hospital is situated right next to the prefabricated buildings "Herlevhuse", (behind the hospital in the picture), which were built at the end of the 1940s as an emergency solution during the first post-war years' extensive lack of housing.

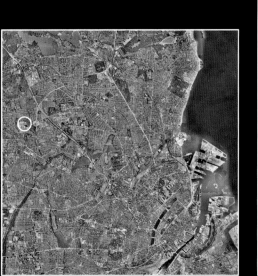

Nybro and Frederiksdal

Northern Zealand's green areas have "always" had a magnetic effect on the city's upper classes.

The royal family led the way with various pleasure palaces in the country, and from the 18th century, the richer part of the middle classes began in earnest to build country houses close to forests and beaches. Like in the area at Frederiksdal.

In the picture below, a narrow canal connects the lake of Bagsværd Sø (bottom right) with the lake of Lyngby Sø (top right). Nybro ensures that the traffic on the Nybrovej road can pass Marienborg (middle of the picture), (see pages 232-233) and continue out of the lower left corner of the picture past Sofienholm (outside the picture) towards Frederiksdal. The fortification canal,

which leads the water in the stream of Mølleåen from the lake of Furesøen and Frederiksdal into the lake of Lyngby Sø, is hidden behind the trees at the left.

In the picture at the bottom of the opposite page, the view has been reversed. Canoeists are enjoying themselves in the fortification canal's outlet into the lake of Lyngby Sø. The bridge at the top of the picture connects Nybro (to the left outside the picture) with Lyngby Åmose. A little further to the north-west in the forest we find Frederiksdal Palace (picture at the top of the opposite page).

The palace was built by the first count Schulin in 1744-45 and got its present rococo appearance in 1752-53. The palace is still owned by the Schulin family.

Marienborg

Supreme court attorney Christian Ludvig David left Marienborg to the Danish state in 1960. The beautiful country house was made available to the incumbent prime minister to provide the setting for events of a representative nature and as a summer residence.

Marienborg was built around 1745 as a country house for the director of Asiatisk Kompagni, Olfert Fisher (father of the naval hero to be) and got its present appearance in the 1760s. Marienborg is situated close to the Nybrovej road (to the right in the picture), and the surrounding park slopes towards the lake of Lyngby Sø at the top of the picture. The prime minister's private quarters are in the wing to the right of the main building and has been used to varying degrees by the respective prime ministers during the past almost 50 years. The main building is used for meetings, parties and official events that are hosted by the prime minister and his or her spouse. Marienborg is probably best known by the public in connection with the prime minister's new year speech, which is broadcast from the work room on the first floor.

Frilandsmuseet
– an open air museum

"Enjoy the countryside in the middle of the city" is the slogan of Frilandsmuseet, which is one of the world's oldest and largest open air museums. It was established by Bernhard Olsen in 1897 as Dansk Folkemuseum in the park of Kongens Have and was moved in 1901 to an area in Lyngby close to Sorgenfri Palace.

We are above the oldest part of the museum with the old yellow main building at the road of Kongevejen at the bottom of the picture. The whitewashed farm houses in the picture originate from Lolland-Falster and Zealand. The close to 100 buildings are organised by region in village-like formations or lie isolated, depending on their original location in the Danish countryside. The museum area has been much extended through the years and today it covers 36 hectares stretching towards the stream of Mølleåen (outside the top of the picture) and north towards Brede (diagonally from the upper left corner).

All the buildings have been carefully disassembled piece by piece at their original locations and reassembled equally carefully at the museum. With their Spartan furniture, the farm houses illustrate life in the country in Denmark in the period from 1700 to about 1900. Frilandsmuseet, which today belongs under the Danish National Museum, is not only a gem of cultural history, but also a green oasis close to the city.

55°46'43.51"N 12°29'48.74"E

Sorgenfri Palace

Sorgenfri Slot lies withdrawn from the Kongevejen road in an area sloping towards the stream of Mølleåen (outside the top of the picture). The palace was erected at the beginning of the 18th century as the residence of count Carl Ahlefeldt and was rebuilt in 1756 in rococo style. At that occasion it was also provided with the characteristic copper clad tower. In the 1790s the buildings were modernised once more, now in the style of New Classicism.

The palace is situated in a large park that was originally established according to the baroque style, but at the beginning of the 19th century it was restructured so as to be an English garden in accordance with the fashion of that time. The long white ladies' wing to the right in the picture was previously used by the royal staff, whereas the gentlemen's building (bottom right) and the staples (bottom left) set the frame for the palace complex towards the Kongevejen road.

The palace has been owned by the king for two periods.

In 1730 Christian VI acquired Sorgenfri as a residence for the crown prince, the later Frederik V. The later Christian VIII also lived in the palace, which in 1898 was made available to prince Christian (Christian X) and his wife Alexandrine. For the next 50 years the palace had its heyday as a summer residence for the royal couple (1912-1947) with royal Danish life guards posted at the main entrance at Kongevejen. The princes Frederik (Frederik IX) and Knud (heir presumptive) were thus born at the palace, which after the death of Christian X in 1947 served as a home for prince Knud and princess Caroline Mathilde until his death in 1995. The palace building is not being used at present.

Charlottenlund Palace

Charlottenlund Palace is hiding under the trees of the palace garden that are beginning to assume the colours of autumn.

The palace's history dates back to the establishment of a hunting lodge at the place in 1663. In 1690, the royal family built the pleasure palace Gyldenlund instead. It was rebuilt in 1730 by Christian VI's sister Charlotte Amalie, who named the palace after herself: Charlottenlund.

The palace has been used by various members of the royal family as a summer residence, and at the beginning of the 19th century, the palace park was more popular with Copenhageners as a place for excursions than the Dyrehaven park.

Crown prince Frederik (later Frederik VIII) moved in in 1869, and here he led a boring life with his very religious wife Lovisa, who as ex-queen stayed here during the summer until her death in 1926. Since the 1930s, the palace has been the headquarters of the Danish Institute for Fisheries Research.

A corner of the palace park lends space to Denmark's Aquarium.

55°46'32.75"N   12°34'34.45"E

The Bakken amusement park

Bakken is the world's oldest amusement park; its history is said to date back to 1583 when Kirsten Piil found a curative spring at the place. (The spring still spouts merrily right outside the left side of the picture). Quickly, the area came to attract Copenhageners in the summer time, and street performers and stalls with food and drink soon followed. In the 19th century, Bakken started to gets its present character, and the association of stall holders was formed in 1885. The stall holders are still a characteristic feature of Bakken, even though there are few stalls nowadays. Bakken is not a company, but a place where the many stall holders run their businesses in the open air, offering food and drink, song and music, performances or neck-

breaking challenges in running or flying attractions. And there is no entrance fee! The classic Bakken attractions include Sangerindepavillonen – the singing ladies' pavilion, the big rollercoaster from 1932, Pjerrot, the open air stage and the revue Cirkusrevyen in the green tent to the right on Bakken. Attractions come and go, but still Bakken has kept its special popular atmosphere, which is especially attractive on an early summer Sunday when the trees are covered in light green.

A little north of Bakken we find Peter Liep's restaurant (at the top of the picture). The former forest officer Peter Liep opened his eatery in 1888. The house burned in 1915, and the present building opened as a restaurant in 1917.

Hubertus

In the Dyrehaven forest north of Copenhagen, the bugles sound, red jackets contrast the autumn colours, the riders scale the hurdles and hurry on towards the Eremitage palace.

Here, the riders rest before the second half where a numerous audience at the pond of Magasindammen expectantly awaits the field's scaling of the pond with its compulsory contact with the wet element for the most unfortunate participants. Two riders with foxtails attached to their outfit lead the way, acting "prey" in front of the hurrying participants.

The performance makes you think of an English manor in the 19th century.

We are attending the Hubertus hunt

Saint Hubertus is the patron of the hunters. Every year since its establishment in 1900, the riding club Sportsrideklubber has arranged this traditional "hunt" on the first Sunday in November. It is a kind of continuation of the traditional hunt with hounds for which Dyrehaven was established during the time of despotism. Nowadays, the game can take it more easily (see pages 246-247).

The Hubertus hunt takes place in the area around the Eremitage Palace (see next page), which was erected 1734-36 a the highest point in Dyrehaven. The palace was designed by one of the leading architects at the time, Lauritz de Thurau, for Christian VI. It is still used occasionally by the royal family

55°47'42.71"N 12°34'17.17"E

248 55'46'43.26"N 12'35'34.42"E

Bellevue

We are on the beach of beaches in the Copenhagen area. Bellevue at Klampenborg close to the Dyrehaven forest north of the city. The area was inaugurated as a beach park actually designed by an architect in 1932.

The buildings to be used for changing, bathing, etc. were designed by the young Arne Jacobsen, who was also behind the lifeguard towers, one of which is in a somewhat scruffy condition.

Originally, Bellevue was divided into a payment beach (the northern beach) and a free beach (the southern beach) for the general public that usually came from the south! The class division was emphasized by the fence that separated the beaches. The beach sections are said still to be divided according to social criteria to some degree, but also in consideration of children and prams, ball games and sexual orientation! Even though the fence has been long gone.

Index